WESLEY CARR

Tested by the Cross

FOREWORD BY
THE ARCHBISHOP OF CANTERBURY

Fount
An Imprint of HarperCollins*Publishers*

Fount Paperbacks is an Imprint of
HarperCollins*Religious*
Part of HarperCollins*Publishers*
77–85 Fulham Palace Road, London W6 8JB

First published in Great Britain
in 1992 by Fount Paperbacks

1 3 5 7 9 10 8 6 4 2

Copyright © 1992 Wesley Carr

Wesley Carr asserts the moral right to be
identified as the author of this work

A catalogue record for this book is
available from the British Library

ISBN 0 00 627626-1

Printed and bound in Great Britain by
HarperCollinsManufacturing Glasgow

Conditions of Sale
This book is sold subject to the condition
that it shall not, by way of trade or otherwise,
be lent, re-sold, hired out or otherwise circulated
without the publisher's prior consent in any form of
binding or cover other than that in which it is
published and without a similar condition
including this condition being imposed
on the subsequent purchaser.

All rights reserved. No part of this publication
may be reproduced, stored in a retrieval system,
or transmitted, in any form or by any means,
electronic, mechanical, photocopying,
recording or otherwise, without the prior
permission of the publishers.

CONTENTS

For Mary and John
with thanks for
wisdom, support and friendship

ACKNOWLEDGEMENTS

Quotations from scripture are from memory or my own translation. I acknowledge the use of the following copyright material:

Macmillan London Ltd for lines from *Pilgrimages* by R. S. Thomas.

The estate of Wilfred Owen and Chatto and Windus for lines from *At a Calvary near Ancre*, *The Next War* and *The Parable of the Old Man and the Young* in Jon Stallworth (ed), *The Poems of Wilfred Owen*.

Faber and Faber Ltd for lines from *The Transfiguration* by Edwin Muir and a passage from *Free Fall* by William Golding.

Constable and Co Ltd for lines from *Peter Abelard* by Helen Waddell.

Dedalus Press for lines from *The Chosen Garden* by Michael O'Siadhal.

FOREWORD

by the Archbishop of Canterbury

This is not an easy book. But a soft and comfortable book about the Cross would not be worth reading. Wesley Carr has resisted the common temptation to turn a faith focused on a crucified Lord into a comfortable religion. Our experience of suffering and evil, power and weakness, freedom and loss, cries out for more than comfort. We are met by a God who does not say that our experience is an illusion and all is well, but one who breaks into our experience through the Cross.

The meaning of what God does through the Cross of Christ is inexhaustible. Perhaps that's why, as Wesley Carr points out, no single doctrine of the Cross has ever been defined by the Church to the exclusion of all others. In the Nicene creed we simply recite the facts of the story and say Christ "was crucified under Pontius Pilate; he suffered death and was buried". It is for each of us to explore the meaning of his death and be tested by what it reveals about God and the reality of his nature.

Christians have done this instinctively down the ages. Yet during Lent, many of us seek to inform those instincts, to test them and expand our understanding of the faith we hold. I believe this book will serve that purpose admirably. It is not an easy read. But it is an immensely rewarding and stimulating contribution to Christian thinking.

✝ George Cantuar

INTRODUCTION

If you ask people to sing about or draw a picture of the Christian message, one emblem always comes through. As a symbol the cross is much older than Christianity. But now it has become supremely Christian. It was scrawled in the catacombs. The Emperor Constantine believed he saw it in the sky. That sign converted him and changed the history of the world.

Many Christians, from worshippers to footballers, still instinctively make the sign of the cross at key moments. Even in churches where preachers fulminate against images, a cross can usually be seen somewhere. It has sustained martyrs and spurred on crusaders and inquisitors. It stands for some of the Church's greatest glories and for moments of its deepest shame.

Martin Luther gives us the motto for this Lent book: "The cross puts everything to the test. Blessed is he who understands."[1] It is not just that we look at the cross, but it scrutinizes our Christian belief, including what we believe about the cross itself. Nothing is more secure within the Christian tradition than the crucifixion. It is in the creeds and cannot be moved: "He was crucified under Pontius Pilate."

Yet although the theme of the cross is the core of Christianity, the Church has never decreed any one doctrine of that cross as orthodox. Other parts of Christian belief – God, the incarnation, the resurrection, the Trinity – have been turned into dogmas. But what the cross is about has not been formally defined. It remains first a story not a doctrine. That is also why, central as it is to the Christian faith, it still impresses itself on non-believers.

The Christian Gospel is rich and therefore complex. Some today argue that, if we are to communicate the Gospel, we should make it simple. Yet "simple" belief often treats people as simpletons. For some that may be a way of life; for a few more it may become an occasional relaxation; but for most it will quickly be felt demeaning. The mark of a genuine religious quest is the search for undogmatic certainty. We need conviction that religion and its concerns matter. But we also need sufficient diffidence to give people space to explore it for themselves.

The cross, as core of the Christian faith and universal symbol, does just this. Belief in it is a central Christian conviction. But because the Church has remained formally undogmatic about it, it is always open to be explored by anyone. The cross is never an easy topic for meditation and study. But the annual wrestle with it should be part of every Christian's Lenten discipline.

In this book I have tried to explore how the cross relates to our modern life. In each age it needs to be re-interpreted. As new ways of thinking about mankind and God develop, so we have to rethink the cross, which speaks about our lives and God's. Our age is especially marked by great interest in and learning about ourselves. We have to take these new concerns and insights into our Christian thinking. That is always a struggle. So this book is not always easy. But it is an invitation to engage again seriously with the heart of the Christian faith, to test it and be tested by it.

Even before we begin we have to recognize that all our thinking about the cross will be inadequate. The ancient images are part of the way we experience the cross. These old pictures have been handed down and can still be useful to us. But they hinder us when one of them is treated as if it were the only way of thinking about the crucifixion. For example, judgement is a permanent theme of the cross. So theories based on crime, punishment and forgiveness still have drawing power. In contrast there is Peter Abelard's vision of a loving God, to which we shall come in chapter 5. This still attracts us because we, like Abelard, know the power of passionate love. Both themes are alive in today's world and linked with the cross.

Down the ages people have discovered that the cross cannot endure being overlaid with theory. In the end we always come to it with our imaginations. By nature we long to be sure about things. We like to believe that we can know exactly what happened, when, where, how and why. So if we are to use our imaginations, we need setting free from this longing to be certain. The Church's instinct not to endorse any one theory about the crucifixion confirms the way in which the cross judges our eagerness for certainty about God, ourselves and the world. From the cross we learn that we have to live, not with knowing but with believing.

The cross is also about what God achieves. Many claims are made for what God does in the cross: the world is changed; sin is overcome; death is vanquished. Whatever the case, the story of the cross is about change. The phrase "the work of Christ" has sometimes been used to refer to his passion and death. It contrasts with studies of his life and ministry – "the person of Christ". Who Jesus Christ is and what he stands for cannot be known apart from what God does through the cross. The first Christians seemed to know this. The Passion narratives are by far the longest sagas in the gospels. It is likely that these were assembled before the rest of the story. The cross and resurrection become the lenses through which we all, writers and readers, view Jesus.

Finally, there is pain and suffering. People from time to time have questioned whether Jesus really suffered and died. Perhaps he was so holy that he only seemed to suffer. Since he was God's son, he only appeared to die. But no proposal about the cross which has diminished the suffering or denied the death has lasted long. The suffering was real. Worshippers and artists alike have drawn on this theme. The gospel writers do not under-estimate the physical pain of crucifixion. But neither do they dwell morbidly on it. For them the pain is part of the profound cost to God of dealing with evil, sin and forgiveness.

Whatever else we do when thinking about the cross, we cannot escape these issues. They will keep coming back in this book. But we should note that none of this is restricted to Christians. How we use ancient images, how to live with uncertainty when longing for assurance, what it means to change the world (or at least ourselves), and what is the cost of any achievement, are not private issues for religious people. They run through all life. The first cross stood on a hill for all to see. So the cross remains a public story for all people, never the doctrine of a few.

Most of us have favourite books. Ideas from them stay with us long after we have forgotten the details. For me Jurgen Moltmann's *The Crucified God* is one such. It appeared when the old, once powerful theories felt too remote to help. Moltmann combined learning with his own testimony and passion for his subject. He emphasized the profound injustice of Jesus's death. He brought home how loathsome a crucified man was to God and people. And he explored how Christ's cross not only judges us but also passes a verdict on God himself.

Two other authors deserve mention. W. H. Vanstone's *The Stature of Waiting*, like his earlier *Love's Endeavour, Love's Expense*, challenges casual study of Scripture. Paul Fiddes in his *Past Event and Present Salvation: The Christian Idea of Atonement* has helped me with the question of how our salvation in the present can depend upon a past event. I am especially indebted for ideas which I have taken up in chapter 2.

Martin Luther's saying emphasizes that for the Christian *everything* is subject to the scrutiny of the cross. Our thinking about ourselves, our thinking about God, our reading of Scripture, our prayer and Lenten study are, therefore, also tested by the idea of the cross. As is this book.

Bristol Cathedral   *Wesley Carr*
1992

NOTES
1. From his Weimar works, quoted in W. van Loewenich, *Luther's Theology of the Cross* (Christian Journals Belfast, 1976)

USING THIS BOOK

Lent for us will be a time for consciously walking the way of the cross. This is how we as Christians through prayer and meditation each year draw closer again to Christ. This book offers one chapter for each week of Lent.

At the head of each chapter a passage of the New Testament is recommended. Over the centuries many ideas have gathered around the cross. Most of us probably remember more from hymns that we have sung than directly from the text of the gospels. So, as we think about the issues which the cross raises, we always need to keep the story as first told in the front of our minds. Each week you are invited to get back to basics and probe the suggested passage. To help that study a few notes are offered.

The first three chapters are about the way in which the cross tests some of the basic dilemmas of our lives as human beings – how we live with our neighbour; how we order our personal lives; how we cope in a tormented world. But as we draw nearer to Holy Week, so the question becomes more awesome: does this cross test God himself? We begin to see that the death of Christ not only summons us to a particular way of life. Because God is there at work, it also becomes an invitation to examine God himself.

The book also makes a Lent study course. A study group might find it helpful to go about it this way. Try to keep the group to no more than twelve people, preferably slightly smaller. Members should always read the chapter before attending. It does not matter whether they understand everything or not. The important thing is that everyone should have the same material in mind. Each member should also be asked to jot down not more than two notes in reply to the following questions:

What struck me as new?
What was I reminded of that I had forgotten?
What did I not understand?
What do I believe is important for others from this?

When the group meets the first thing to do is list the answers and questions without any discussion or explanation. This is a short exercise, taking only a little time. Many points will probably overlap, and often only one or two major themes will stand out.

Next, read the New Testament passage and spend a short while thinking about the aspects of the cross which are stressed there. That should give everyone a common focus on the cross during the discussion. The group could use the questions suggested at the end of each chapter.

Make sure there is half an hour at the end. Use this to run through the list created at the beginning. Has any light been thrown on any of these topics, especially any that stood out as common to almost everyone? Finally, re-read without comment or discussion the Bible passage, meditate and pray.

CHAPTER 1

PATRICK BATEMAN'S STORY

Loving My Neighbour

Matthew 26:1–35
From the Plot to Peter's Denial

Each account of the Passion tells the story and puts a slant on it. The writers invite us to share their vision of the way that God works. Matthew sees God's promises in the Old Testament being fulfilled in every part of Jesus' life and death. He attaches texts to events. In this way he emphasizes God's control. Jesus obediently carries out God's will. **Not during the Feast** (*v.* 5) seems to contradict what actually happened. There are problems about the timing of these events. This is an example of the vision taking priority over precise history. Jesus' anointing (*vv.* 6–13) is interpreted as preparation for burial. But Matthew may also wish us to have a second theme in mind. The title "Christ" means "the anointed one", that is, someone chosen by God. So Jesus does God's will, in this case by being prepared to die. **Thirty silver coins** (*v.* 15) is a paltry sum. According to Exodus 21:32 it is what a man must pay if his ox has killed the slave of another. By the time of Jesus it was worth far less. During the betrayal Matthew stresses (*v.* 23) the deceitful action of Jesus' friend. **You have said so** (*v.* 25) is not subtle: it just means "Yes". In his account of the Last Supper Matthew underscores the future (*v.* 29). His Jesus is a pioneer who goes before his disciples. He opens up a new way of life. The **hymn** (*v.* 30) at the end of the Passover was the second part of Psalms 115–118. Unlike Mark, Matthew makes it clear that Jesus' sufferings will be the cause of the disciples' doubt and failure (*v.* 31). He again claims God's deep involvement in Christ's passion by changing the words in the quotation from Zechariah 13:7. The original is a sort of proverb: "Strike the shepherd . . . ". He alters it to **I will strike the shepherd,** so making God responsible. For the same reason, perhaps, he also introduces the first mention of the resurrection in this chapter: **After I have been raised I will go ahead of you** (*v.* 32). Peter's disowning of Jesus contrasts with Matthew's earlier stress on his importance to God. Peter was the rock on which the church will be founded and which even death will not be able to overcome (Matthew 16:18). The Romans called the time between midnight and 3 a.m. "cock crow".

CHAPTER 1

God is Love

The first prize I ever won was awarded at Sunday School for colouring the text "God is love". Generations of children have done the same, painting or embroidering these three words from 1 John. If you asked people what was the basic Christian idea, they would probably come up with something like "God is love".

When candidates for ordination are interviewed, they are always asked about the Gospel. What do they believe? Can they express it or at least give an outline? The answers vary. Everyone has their own testimony. But without fail they will speak of God's love, whether for them or for the world. Some may talk about a personal moment when they had an overwhelming sense of this love. Some will have come to it through the care shown to them by someone else. Some will hold it as a vision for an ideal world.

We might expect ordinands to talk like this. But the same is true of many who would not claim to be particularly Christian. Their sense of Christianity is roughly that God loves us and so we ought to love one another.

Major disasters disturb many people, not just those directly involved. At such times people who do not believe in God, as well as others who are unsure about whether to or not, express their beliefs about God. How, they ask, can he (in whom we do not, of course, believe) allow such terrible

21

things to happen? They assume that God is, or ought to be, kind and merciful – in a word, loving.

Believers have their religious experiences. Others hold to their rough and ready belief in God. Atheists live with their confusion. But all of us, whatever our belief, today make another assumption. We treat love as though it were essentially a feeling. Like all feelings it may then turn out to be temporary. This accounts for the banal recipes which are supposed to transform the world. "Love makes the world go round", which ends up as a soft drink advertisement for "perfect harmony". Some Christians share this sort of thinking. Slogans in their cars offer slick answers to everyone's need. One even copies the Coca Cola logo, changing the message to "Jesus is the Real Thing".

To be foolish in proclaiming the Gospel is not new. Eagerness has frequently led Christians to behave strangely and even stupidly. But God seems able to cope with us. Even the Church manages to survive. But there is a danger. We may come to believe that we possess a scheme for saving the world: "If only people loved everybody else, as I do because God loves me, the world would be a better place." Gradually rich ideas of love are reduced to mutual fondness.

This can have serious effects. For example, ministers' pastoral work degenerates into easy encouragement. With a smile pastors exhort people to love God, love themselves and love their neighbour. There we have the caricature vicar. He is mildly funny. We know that he means well. But we also know in our hearts that all our relationships are more of a struggle than his niceness implies. There is no easy way of living with one another.

Whether we are thinking about the family, the nation,

or even the world, life together is fraught. When we propose simplistic solutions based on vague notions of affection, it is not surprising that people think Christianity is tired. The title (not so much the content) of a book says it all: *I'm OK – You're OK.*[1] Under the guise of loving them we can undervalue people.

Yet in spite of these problems, love remains a central theme in Christian belief. We claim, for example, that the cross demonstrates what God's love is like; that it shows the lengths to which he will go; and that it points to a purer form of love than ours. This view emphasizes self-giving. But even this ideal is today under scrutiny. Is acting for others without regard for ourselves still possible?

Feminist thinking, for example, has pointed out how all of us, especially men, expect women to demonstrate self-giving. We all talk of such love but look to them to live it. And when they do, they are exploited and required to be compliant. Many people today doubt whether anyone can genuinely act in a purely generous way. Self-interest always lurks somewhere. But whatever we think of this, all of us have become more aware of how both parties in any relationship affect each other. "God is love" once seemed a simple truth. It turns out to be less obvious than we had thought.

Restricted loving

It has become hard to know what is involved in loving another person. Overwhelming feelings make it difficult to be sure. Love, they say, is blind. It clouds our judgement. Thank goodness. Life would be inhuman if everything were analysed and nothing felt. But love also brings us into contact with others. And then we discover reponsibilities which we cannot ignore. When the other person, our neighbour, is someone who returns our affection, we can learn with them what is required of both of us.

Love is also about choice. The amazed lover asks his loved one why of all people she chose him. Lovers return again and again to this question. The same is true of God's love. We experience it as his choosing us. We affirm this repeatedly through worship. The message that God has chosen us and loves us is proclaimed. We respond by choosing – that is, worshipping – him.

But what when we are told to love our neighbours but do not choose them? This has been a problem since people were first thrown together in communities. But these days it has become more acute. Our horizons have been expanded. The enlarged world raises new questions. Our neighbours now become those we see but can never meet – starving, distressed, diseased people. Our feelings of concern are matched by a sense of our impotence.

What is love in this maze of connections? Philo, a contemporary of Jesus, spoke like him. There are, he said, two fundamental doctrines, "one of duty to God, as shown by piety and holiness, one of duty to men, as shown by humanity and justice".[2] The ideal is noble. But it stretches beyond our own resources to act. We cannot even imagine these other people's worlds. So we are deprived of choice, resource and ability. The command to love our neighbour becomes destructive. We feel that we ought to work for the good of all our neighbours; but whenever we try to love others our inability to do so is exposed.

Faced by this predicament we withdraw into familiar

worlds. We restrict love to mutual affection. Life assurance societies are often "mutual". It means that all members have an interest in each other's life. All pay premiums; all will eventually make claims. The members belong in order to benefit one another. Our idea of love can develop like this. It becomes a matter of dealing with people who we know can respond.

This has happened even in Christian worship. Giving the Peace is an ancient ritual which has been recovered in recent years. Services in various churches often include some sort of greeting. We extend the Peace as a sign that we are brought together by God's gift of himself. It also symbolizes the way that we are reconciled with those we have offended. The person we greet represents all these others to us. So by custom he or she should be someone we do not know. But today embracing friends replaces greeting the stranger or the estranged. Husband kisses wife; members of the congregation assure each other of their undying affection "in the Lord". Love is reduced to mutual affection between friends.

Narcissus

Under the guise of being concerned for – that is loving – our neighbours, we can fall into the trap of loving ourselves. Narcissus was a beautiful young man. One day he glimpsed himself reflected in a pool. He fell passionately in love with this reflection. Day by day he pined for it. Eventually he wasted away and was changed into a beautiful, fragile flower.

His name gives us one of today's catch words – narcissism. We treat this as if it were a sort of selfishness. Narcissists fall in love with themselves and exclude others. But the myth is truer to real life. Narcissus did not adore himself. He was gazing into a pool and saw a reflection of himself. He loved his image, not himself. Self-love did not kill Narcissus. He adored something that did not really exist but that he hoped might. He needed to keep the one he loved as a copy of himself.

Narcissus' love affair seemed perfect. There was no difference between himself and his beloved. The two were genuinely one. But there was, therefore, no real relationship between the two of them. The object of his love could never become someone challenging, enlivening and different. Narcissus had no incentive to live with change. He had every reason to keep things fixed.

The outcome is obvious to us. The relationship between Narcissus and the image seemed intimate and, at least to him, mutual. But it was doomed to destroy them both, because the reflection could not be anything other than what Narcissus was. And, of course, when Narcissus died, so did his image.

Today we have developed a style of casual intimacy like that of Narcissus. Take a trivial example. We use first names freely, almost instinctively. A person's first name was once a gift. You received permission to say it. But now its use has become the norm. Relationships on radio and television are ephemeral. Formality has relaxed. Brief interviews are framed in immediate intimacy. We have abolished the process of being progressively invited to draw closer.

Like any change this one has its positive side. We are well rid of some of the stranger class differences that underlay the older ways of behaving. But these conventions had one important function. They helped people, especially at first, to know where they stood. By contrast presumed intimacy makes us uncertain of who we are expected to be.

This has a curious outcome. Today's relationships have apparently become more intimate. In practice, however, we become more and more aware of ourselves and less of others. The casual use of names diminishes space for discovering one another. So we cease to bother. But anxiety about myself increases. Am I doing it right? Is my behaviour giving wrong signals?

Industries are founded on this worry. Advertising offers cosmetic reassurance – "You can be the beautiful person that you know is hiding inside." Others offer counselling – "Discover the real you and what is inhibiting the expression of your true self". But the more these solutions are offered, the more anxious we become.

Patrick Bateman's Story

Patrick Bateman is the central character in Bret Easton Ellis' novel *American Psycho*. He is a twenty-six-year-old New Yorker who seems to have everything. Handsome, charming and intelligent, day by day he earns staggering sums on Wall Street. His consumerist lifestyle matches his income. Anything he wants, he can buy. So long as it has a fashionable brand name, he does so. Patrick uses his friends as a mirror in which to adore himself. They have long and serious discussions about how to look, what to do, where to go, whom to recognize. Patrick has everything, people as well as things.

But there is another side. Patrick Bateman is a psychopath. He murders people and abuses his victims both before and after killing them. His violence becomes increasingly sadistic and obscene. But he is not caught, and his double life continues to the end.

This novel is not for the squeamish. Some consider it pornographic but that, I think, is superficial. The true horror is that Patrick is not obviously appalling. He easily fits into his world and ours. Because he does not stand out, the monstrosity of a society which is no longer offended by greed and disturbed by suffering is exposed.

Patrick is not obviously terrible. The clue to him is simple: like many of us, Patrick needs to make everything and everyone around him just right. His success, his acquisitiveness and his murderous behaviour are aspects of his self–love. So Patrick has to possess everything and everyone so as to put them into the proper order in relation to himself. He ends up devouring things and people alike.

He is not unthinking or unfeeling. Throughout the story he reflects on his lifestyle. He believes that he discovers his real self through consumption and destruction. But as he acquires more, his murders become increasingly extravagant. He adores himself so much that he can justify his abuse and murders. But his narcissism is steadily leading him to murder others and so he is destroying himself.

At the end of the novel Patrick is sitting with some friends in Harry's bar. He thinks about life and whether it has any meaning. But even when we leave him he is still preoccupied with things being correct and properly ordered:

And above one of the doors covered by red velvet drapes in Harry's is a sign and on the sign in letters that match the drape's color are the words THIS IS NOT AN EXIT.[3]

Patrick has no way of making any sense of his life. But he is worried about this. He cannot discover who he is, because he lives in a world where everyone and everything is an object. He is not unloving. But he has no means of understanding relationships. He is casually intimate with things, friends and victims, as he searches for who he is himself.

We could hope that we are different. Patrick Bateman is horrific. We may reckon him sick. He is easy to dislike. But he presents us with more than a macabre lifestyle. Meeting him, we question what we mean by love, what it is to care for anyone, and who is truly my neighbour.

When Jesus told us to love God and love our neighbour, he was not saying anything new. His audience knew what he was talking about. They already had an idea of what he meant when he spoke of "God" and "neighbour". Today, however, we no longer have shared ideas of God and neighbour, ourselves and others. So we cannot discover how to love and care by hearing again the old recipes, however true they may be.

But there is more to the Christian message than repeating Jesus' teaching. It is about what we can make of our life in the light of the story of his life, death and resurrection. In the story of the cross, we find this already beginning, as we hear the stories of those who lived out there what they believed.

Narcissism: the story of Judas

Jesus is obviously central to the crucifixion story. The group of disciples is also prominent and two, Peter and Judas, are key individuals. Judas' role is second only to that of Jesus. The passion begins with him.

Throughout history Judas has been maligned as the one who betrayed Jesus. Christians have forever damned him. Preachers speculate about him. They confidently attribute to him motives of which he was probably unaware and innocent. W. H. Vanstone describes how he heard sermons as a young man which always disappointed him.

> The preachers all seemed to assume that it mattered a great deal, for they used of Judas such phrases as "he sent his Master to His death"; "he had Jesus' blood on his hands"; "through his greed or resentment or disillusion he became guilty of the greatest crime in history".[4]

But they rarely, if ever, asked why what Judas did actually mattered. It may have been wrong, but did it seriously affect the course of events?

The gospels offer a consistent picture of Judas. He is no wan Narcissus, gazing at his own reflection. Judas is active, resolute and effective. He deals with the priests; he arranges Jesus' betrayal; he decides on the sign of a kiss; and when it is all over he hangs himself. Far from being a robot, Judas represents a very human sort of responsibility. He has a vision of what might be and what ought to be. He tries to bring it about. His is an independent mind. When he acts, he is decisive. No one now wishes to be called "Judas". But most of us would like to be such a character.

Judas thought of himself as a man to be reckoned with. But his behaviour is confused. For example, why did he need to identify Jesus in the Garden of Gethsemane? It was unnecessary. Jesus was well enough known by that stage. So the kiss does not point Jesus out. It is a sign of love, honour, affection and longed-for intimacy. As Judas kisses Jesus he draws him to himself. He embraces all that he wishes himself to be and has found he cannot be.

Judas exposes what happens when we act on the basis of being in love with our own image. We have already seen how narcissism must destroy us. But the story of Narcissus does not show how it also devastates others. Someone always has to bear the impact of our concern with ourselves and our image. Judas Iscariot was not the only one to die that Good Friday. Three others are also killed: the two bandits and Jesus.

We like today to believe that our behaviour can be private. It is not, or at least should not be, of any concern to others. But the story of Judas gives the lie to this naive belief. Like Patrick Bateman he discovered that narcissistic behaviour is never a private matter. Certainly it is not harmless.

But can anything be done? The question for Judas is: can he ever be forgiven? The poet Edwin Muir has written about the transfiguration. In the gospels this story tells how three chosen disciples were given a vision of Jesus's hidden glory. For a split second they saw him with the heavenly figures of Moses and Elijah. They are overwhelmed. The poet, however, imagines more. He describes how for a moment the world was transformed. Everything for once fell perfectly into place. The mystery of the hidden order of the universe was disclosed. One secret concerns Judas:

And Judas damned take his long journey backward
From darkness into light and be a child
Beside his mother's knee, and the betrayal
Be quite undone and never more be done.[5]

31

We tend to regard forgiveness as something that happens between two people. If I wrong you, you may forgive me; I may accept your forgiveness. It sounds plausible. But Judas and the cross which he helped bring about test such an ordinary belief. They prove that it is never a purely personal matter to restore relationships.

God occasionally discloses the web of connections which makes up the world. We see that what happens between you and me affects more than the two of us alone. The impact is not even confined to those around us. We are part of a world which is greater than we know. So if we change, everything around us is in some way also altered, even if it is not always obvious.

Our narcissistic tendencies encourage us to believe that our relationships only affect two, or at most a few, people or groups. But the story of Judas demonstrates that no relationship, even the most intimate, can be isolated like this. Every act of forgiveness may restore closeness between you and me. But there is always more: it is also another restructuring of God's world.

Edwin Muir could have pictured Judas going back to the betrayal or the crucifixion that resulted. It is, after all, surely for those that he needs forgiving. Certainly it is for these acts that Christians have judged Judas. But unlike the preachers, the poet takes us with Judas past Gethsemane and the cross all the way to his mother's knee. We discover that when Judas is forgiven for betraying Jesus, whatever went wrong in his past before that moment is also re-ordered. All the wrongs prior to the betrayal are dealt with. Then the betrayal, coming in a sequence, is "quite undone and never more to be done".

Because Judas is forgiven for one act, all his life is changed. That includes his earlier behaviour. And because of this, all his relationships are also in some way re-ordered. Narcissism can be fatal. But it is not inevitable. We can be changed.

Intimacy: The story of Peter

Judas became the damned disciple. Peter has risen to the top of the Christian ladder. But his story is as rich for us as that of Judas. While Jesus taught in Galilee and was on his journey to Jerusalem, Peter was one of the most active disciples. He looks strong. He is the leader on whom others can rely. Eventually he loftily claims that Jesus can confidently trust him too. Others may abandon him; Peter never will. He patronizes Jesus and the disciples with his determination and apparent strength. But underneath he remains what he has always been: Peter is really the most dependent disciple. He relies more heavily that he knows on Jesus. Time after time he discovers, but never learns, that he of all the disciples most needs Jesus.

Peter's story on the way to Jerusalem is marked by crumbling self-reliance. He leaps into the water and begins to sink. When Jesus washes the disciples' feet Peter switches from aggressive independence to pathetic confusion. "You will never wash my feet!" he exclaims. "Wash all of me!" He is the impulsive one. His behaviour reinforces his self-image. He is loyal and devoted. But these virtues do little for Jesus. They turn out only to be Peter's way of affirming himself. Strong in commitment, this devoted disciple struggles to remain closest to his master.

But the cross disturbs his complacent claim to intimacy. It turns out to have been more casual than he knew. The

33

cross does not question his strength. Peter is strong. He does not have to become stronger. Jesus has already named him "The Rock". But it scrutinizes how reliable he is. Through what happens at the cross Peter learns that he relies more on Jesus than he realizes. That is a hard, but obvious, lesson.

But there is a further discovery which is more important. Peter is someone who is naturally dependent. He leans on Jesus' leadership. So he tries to get close, to become a special friend and disciple. But his bluster and bravado disguise this aspect of himself from him, and maybe the others. He is in fact afraid of his reliance on Jesus. At the cross, however, he learns that his longing is not necessarily a weakness to be denied. If he will allow them to, other people can use his vulnerability. His need to be supported can work the other way round. When he learns about his own need to rely on Jesus, he can become dependable for others. Then he becomes at last the Rock that Jesus called him.

Perhaps that is why Peter ends up weeping but Judas commits suicide. Judas' self-obsession is exclusive. There is no room in his world for more than Judas and Jesus. By contrast Peter presumes intimacy with Jesus. But he lacks much sense of what this involves.

Yet whatever his faults, Peter's behaviour is never exclusive. He needs other people. The change in him, therefore, is also painful but less drastic than in Judas. Peter learns that weakness can be redeemed. Reformed in the light of the cross, it can be used by others. So he becomes, like his master on the cross, usable by others. As a result he becomes in practice the Rock on which the emerging church is built.

Mutual affection: the story of the disciples

Both Judas and Peter acted out of their love for Jesus. But their stories show what happens when such love becomes casual intimacy. The rest of the disciples illustrate the effect of mutual affection when it gets cut off from the real world.

When Jesus died this group, apart from the women, fled. They ended up huddling together, no doubt looking for mutual support, care and counsel during this time of stress. They were isolated from events outside. Like a committee, synod or even some churches they met to discuss events rather than risk being involved in them.

The disciples may have justified their behaviour to themselves as warm fellowship or even a collaborative, enabling ministry. But the stories of the cross strip away any such deceit. Those who met for mutual benefit missed everything that was important. They did not hear Jesus's final words. They were not witnesses to the cross.

But perhaps most poignantly, although they were disciples, they were not the first to meet the risen Christ. It was those who went out and took a risk who encountered Jesus. The women went to the tomb and the disciples who walked to Emmaus had the first inkling of what the cross might mean. The huddled disciples demonstrate how debilitating mutual fondness becomes.

Through the stories of Judas, Peter and the disciples the cross makes us examine what we mean by love. Today's fashions of casual intimacy and mutual affection are scrutinized. Patrick Bateman, Judas, Peter and the disciples have one thing in common: they all take up defensive attitudes. Patrick's and Judas' narcissism locks us into private worlds where others have no place. Casual intimacy, as Peter shows, may protect our self-esteem. But it cannot genuinely risk inviting another into our lives. And the disciples' mutual affection encourages groups in which benefit is totted up in terms of the members' welfare, not that of others.

We may dignify these ways of behaving as "caring" and even "loving". But once we have seen this range of "loving" we reach this conclusion: the notion of love is not strong enough to stand the hopes we invest in it. Love, a central theme of Christianity, is fragile. We have become more sceptical as we have learned more about ourselves. What we feel and why we behave as we do have been analysed. If these were only theoretical questions we could ignore them and get on with our lives. But theories do not remain cut off from everyday life. They become our popular beliefs.

In the nineteenth century, for example, many thought Sigmund Freud's views on human development wild. They could not believe that these new-fangled ideas could replace the wisdom of the ages. But during our century psychology has been popularized. Parents today are more likely to turn to a book on how to bring up the baby than ask their parents what they did. Popular writing on why we behave as we do abounds. Freud and his pioneering colleagues might not recognize their work. But they have had an indelible influence on everyone.

The way we think about love has changed. We are more alert to feelings and more doubtful whether we can ever know our motives. It is this world that the Christian idea of love, especially as this is demonstrated in the cross of Christ, addresses. Religious people cannot today think about God's love as if it were somehow free from such judgements.

The criticism of any sort of love poses questions to all ideas of love.

Love, trust and handing over

Betrayal is a basic theme running through the stories of Judas, Peter and the disciples. Jesus trusts himself to Judas and welcomes his greeting. But Judas betrays Jesus to be tried and condemned. Jesus trusts himself to Peter. He warns him of the danger of headstrong certitude but does not stand in his way. Peter lets Jesus down by denying him and fleeing. Jesus had expressed confidence in all the disciples by calling them to follow. They respond by abandoning him. They betray all that they have stood for with Jesus during his public ministry.

In English to betray someone is an act of treachery. We disapprove. But the original word in the gospels which is usually translated "betray" is more neutral. It does not necessarily describe a wrong. It simply means "to hand over".

"Handing over" is a prominent theme in the New Testament. Jesus is handed over by Judas to the authorities. Pilate in turn hands Jesus over to be crucified. When St Paul expounds what he understands by the Gospel, he uses the same word. He writes of "the Son of God who loved me and handed over himself for me" (Galatians 2:20); "God did not spare his Son but handed him over for us all" (Romans 8:32). The same theme not surprisingly surfaces in worship. St Paul gives us an early description of the Lord's Supper. This, he says, he received from the Lord. In turn "I also handed it over to you" (1 Corinthians 11:23).

The cross, then, is first the result of a "handing over" rather than a "betrayal". Seen like this, it begins to help us understand what we mean by love. The Christian emphasis has been on love as self-giving. God's love is outgoing and generous to a fault and we are called to copy it. This motif is the motto of hymns and testimonies alike. Christians believe that God is like this and experience him as loving:

> For the love of God is broader
>   than the measure of man's mind;
> And the heart of the Eternal
>   Is most wonderfully kind.[6]

But if we take this as our only image of God's love and ours, we over-simplify what we mean by love and turn it into an impossible ideal. But as we have already seen in the stories of Judas, Peter and the others, the impact of the cross is on our everyday experience. So if, as Christians believe, God supremely demonstrates his love there, it must not be just an ideal but a practical, effective sort of loving.

"Handing over" provides the link between the overwhelming ideal of love and our day to day loving. In the passion story Jesus is surrendered by Judas to the authorities, by Pilate to the crowd, and by the crowd to the soldiers. But when we look underneath the surface of the accounts, we see that Jesus, as he is being handed over, is in fact the one doing the handing over. Jesus trusts himself to Judas and risks himself with Peter. He continues in the same way with Pilate, the priests and the crowd. That is why they all find his behaviour mystifying.

Jesus allows others to make of him what they will, not what he wants. He makes himself "usable". He accepts what others wish to make him and to do to him. And he also bears the consequences of trusting them. Such love is not first a feeling. It is self-giving less in the sense of offering than receiving. By entrusting himself to all these people, Jesus shows how the ideal of love has a practical effect.

We are inclined, when we talk about love, to simplify everything. Love is reduced to intimacy or mutual affection. These feelings get us by in some situations. But in practice we discover that this sort of love is not enough. There were certainly powerful and confused emotions at the crucifixion. At every moment of handing over we have hints of strong feelings in all involved.

But there was more to this handing over than feeling. Love there is exposed also as trust. When we grasp that point, other emotions than lovingness become important. They are as much part of the experience of loving my neighbour. Trust, for instance, involves the noble act of self-giving, with all the generous emotions that it conjures up. But it can also be betrayal, with all the dark feelings connected with that. When we see that love is trust, we acknowledge that it is more complex than our modern simplicities suggest.

There are many pitfalls even in the warmest relationship. Misunderstandings easily occur. Usually when these happen we blame the other person rather than ourselves. The person we have loved seems to become undeserving. We quickly become self-righteous. But when we see that love is essentially trust, we shift from being preoccupied with what we may or may not have given. We become suitably aware of ourselves. We entrusted ourselves to someone. We invited their response. Love seen as trust enables us to discover, as Peter did, how we can be used to bear the trust of others.

The cross demonstrates that genuine love is best thought

of like this. Jesus, together with all the other actors in that drama, show what is involved when we hand ourselves over to others. The cross gives us a new vision of what the command means that we should love both God and our neighbour. The command to love God is not first a call to an emotion. It means embracing a style of living which we draw from God's own expression of what his love means. The test is how usable we are willing to let ourselves be for others. And these "others" are the neighbours whom we are secondly called to love. We certainly will do many things for them. But now we add from the cross that to love our neighbours is also to entrust ourselves to them. That means some risk. For we have to be able to receive people's expectations of us and handle them. Feelings are not denied. But they are put into a new context.

Loving God and my neighbour

What does all this mean in practical terms? In order to trust someone we need some distance from them. Most parents and children at some point play the trust game. The child stands on a stair or a sofa. Daddy says "Jump!" The child hesitates: will she or will she not? She does not know. Father does not know. Both are risking something with each other. Then the child jumps. Father catches. They both laugh with relief. It is a simple enough illustration. But without the little bit of distance from the stair to father's arms, there can be no test of trust for anyone.

Our modern ideas of love stress being close. Obviously love and intimacy go together. But if love is also about entrusting ourselves to others, then giving them space becomes important. To be trusted we also have to distance ourselves enough for them to be able to use us. This may sound uncaring. We are today more used to the idea of drawing close. Caring people talks a lot about "being alongside". We are preoccupied with nearness to one another. So to talk of trust and distance is risky. People may take it to imply a hardened heart; we should leave people to their own devices and see what happens. But distance does not mean abandonment, as the cross makes clear.

In St John's Gospel Jesus says, "When I am lifted up from the earth, I will draw all people to myself" (John 12:32). Here, as always with John, we should read the text on a number of levels. But "lifting up" must first refer to his crucifixion. A cross was raised above people and the victim was separated from them. By being hung up Jesus was literally distanced from people. But a crucified man was also the object of disgust. So Jesus was in another sense also separated from the rest of humankind. Yet, says the writer, by his separation Jesus will draw everyone into a new closeness with him.

Distance is an ingredient in loving trust. It is not the whole. But it is a key, if we are really willing to entrust ourselves to others and allow them to use us. It is through being generous with ourselves that we find we come into greater closeness with people. Distance and closeness, trust and intimacy, then combine in a profound experience of what we call love.

When we see this, we can better deal with another of today's difficulties with love. This is our tendency to manipulate others, especially those to whom we are drawn. Like Narcissus our instinct is to try to make someone we love in our own image. Both Judas and Peter in their different fashions reckoned that they loved Jesus. But each showed this by trying to manipulate him into doing what they thought would be best for him and hence for them. We all do it. Sometimes we are blatant but more often surreptitious. We act powerfully upon someone else. And we protest that it is for their own good.

Christians are notoriously at risk of this error. Without thinking we derive a vision from the Gospel. Because we believe that Gospel, the vision naturally includes ourselves. But we have many other contacts. So we try to make our vision into everyone's. We justify our action by calling it evangelism or mission. At its worst this behaviour leads to forced conversions and even the Inquisition.

John and William worked together. Their families got to know each other. They enjoyed their work and were stimulated by one another's company. One day they were working together in a stressful context. They disagreed. John announced that he had really involved William for his own good. He intended to change aspects of him that he thought needed altering. William argued that he had come in order to work, not to be improved. Discussion became impossible. John could not trust William to be who he was. He wanted a different person, in fact someone with his own supposed virtues. William felt attacked. Trust was lost and their relationship broke down. There was a loss to them both. But even more, others lost the benefit of their work.

We have seen that to act without self-interest is more difficult than we might think. But in the light of the cross, Christians can believe that it is possible. Obviously our motives can never be one hundred per cent known to us and therefore pure. But it does not follow that we have to surrender to the idea that all relationships are in the end self-serving. The perspective of the cross gives us a model of what love involves and how entrusting need never be mere self-concern. For it displays to us how God's entrusting of himself to us is his way of loving us. We need not, therefore, ever try to disguise the basis on which we are offering ourselves as usable by people.

I am often asked what I do as a Dean and what happens at Bristol Cathedral. Given the range of activity in a modern cathedral, any number of answers could be offered. But I always reply, "I (or we) pray for you". This is not especially pious, but it is a true answer. Round the year we pray in the cathedral three times daily without fail. Amid the thousand and one other things, this is something that we can and do guarantee. But this answer is also a small instance of what entrusting and being usable means. They may, if they wish, use our praying. But the response also registers the point that the Cathedral has a godly function. Everything we say and do is a statement about what we believe about God. That said; we trust ourselves to them. They may make of us, and through us of God, what they choose.

This is a simple instance of what Christian loving is about. Things cease to be about me and my behaviour alone. Nor are they just about my neighbour and me. Each moment when we are used, is a moment when God's nature as love is proclaimed.

The cross offers this perspective. The Judas, Peter and Patrick in each of us is given a new vision. So long as I have such a trusting regard for my neighbour I shall be acting lovingly towards him or her, whatever happens. We draw this pattern for our behaviour from the crucified. Without it in this modern world the ideals of love and care will decay. We will drift into diagnosing what is wrong with people, including ourselves. We may categorize and patronize others. The result is that for the best of motives we end up demeaning the one whom we long to love or care for, our neighbour. But the cross stands as a permanent reminder that all our ideas of love need constantly to be checked and tested. And that test comes from our neighbours, whom we love by entrusting ourselves to them.

FOR DISCUSSION

1. "God so loved the world." How does the cross give this statement meaning?

2. Care is a mark both of counselling and of Christian ministry. How do they compare and how do they differ?

3. What in your life or that of your church changes, when trust is seen as the key to love?

CHAPTER 2

SAMMY MOUNTJOY'S DILEMMA

The Fear of Freedom

Matthew 27:1–26
From Trial to Sentence

Matthew and the other writers give the overall impression that the trial of Jesus was conducted in haste. Procedure was disregarded. Once the decision is made in Gethsemane, the process which God has started rushes on. It works through many people. Its appointed end must be reached. Nothing, not even human justice, can hinder it. The **council** (*v*. 1) would have been the Sanhedrin. This was made up of the elders, the present and former chief priests, their families and the scribes. It had 71 members; 23 formed a quorum. **Pontius Pilate** (*v*. 2) governed from 26 to 36 A.D. By contrast with other sources the Gospels are quite kind about him. We only have three accounts of what happened to **Judas**: this one (*vv*. 3–10), Acts 1:18–20, and one in a fragment from the middle of the second century. Matthew links the story in Acts 1:16–20, which was written before his Gospel, with Zechariah 11:12–13. His constant point, however, is to connect stories with Old Testament prophecy and its fulfilment. He compares Judas' remorse with the Council's eagerness to condemn Jesus. When Jesus meets Pilate (*vv*. 11–26) the question of kingship arises. This would have caused the Roman Governor anxiety. The words **King of the Jews** are here spoken by a Gentile from the West. They remind us of the same phrase in the mouths of the Wise Men from the East at Jesus' birth (Matthew 2:2). The custom of releasing a prisoner is only mentioned in the Gospels. Matthew gives the name of **Jesus Barabbas** (*v*. 17). It contrasts with **Jesus Christ**. Pilate's wife (*v*. 19) only appears here. But Matthew is fond of revelation through dreams. He is also determined to make the Jewish people responsible for Jesus' death. The famous story of Pilate washing his hands (*v*. 24) is odd. It was a Jewish custom (Deuteronomy 21:6), not Roman. Here, and in the following verses, Matthew is making a point about God's judgement. It may be included as a warning to Christians: just as Judas met his fate, so too can God's chosen people err and suffer in consequence. Scourging (*v*. 26) was one of the rituals of crucifixion, designed to weaken the condemned man.

CHAPTER 2

Freedom is longed for but feared. I began this chapter in August 1991 during the attempted coup in the USSR. Hour by hour we watched developments in Moscow. Ordinary people gathered to confirm that they would not give up their emancipation. They confronted tanks. They also discovered their new liberty to argue with one another about what it meant to be free.

Nearer home thousands of young people were receiving their A-level results. In limbo between leaving school and the longed for freedom of college life or the beginning of work, they were struggling with their parents, their peers and themselves.

Susan from the age of sixteen had cajoled her parents to let her leave home. If she could get away, she would be able to manage her life. "I want to be me." Her parents pointed out that she was not very good at washing her clothes or making her bed. She had never had to buy food and could scarcely cook. Above all she could never manage her allowance. Susan went to college a long way from home. She quickly learned that the world was not what she expected. The college demanded more work than school. Peer pressure was stronger than that of home. At first she was in disarray. But to her amazement the experience also opened up to her new aspects of herself. Her parents had often told her that she possessed these. She handled personal relationships with skill. So others turned to her for support

49

and help. She still had difficulty with money. There was never enough and she was often in debt. At the end of term she found herself in a dilemma. She longed to return to the familiar home and her parents. But she did not want to take her new self, which had emerged as she had exercised her freedom, back home.

Susan's experience is everyone's. Like the Muscovites and Susan we long for freedom to express what we are. One wants to be "a human being"; the other wishes to be "me". For us all, it is the same terrible freedom. When we are free, then we can express something about ourselves. But do we wish to know?

Frightening freedom

Two leading characters in the saga of the cross reveal that freedom is easily claimed but becomes frightening when exercised. Judas, as we have already seen, uses his freedom of choice. We know little about him and his significance within the group of disciples. His motives for betraying Jesus are uncertain. But in the story one point remains clear: Judas decides for himself what he will do. He exercises his freedom and acts. But in so doing discovered a self which he despised. So he killed himself.

Pilate's story is similar. The system gave a Roman governor great freedom of judicial discretion. It required him to use it responsibly. But in the passion story, faced by Jesus, Barabbas, the crowd, his wife, the conflicting evidence and political pressures, this freedom is too much to bear. Pilate declines into indecision. Finally he abdicates, washing his hands of the whole affair. For one moment he behaves resolutely. He writes the placard to be put above the crucified Jesus: "This is the

King of the Jews". But his resolve is only temporary. According to one tradition he, too, committed suicide.

These are two examples. But the theme of people having and using their own freedom runs through the Gospels. For example, the disciples are free to stay faithful to Jesus or to deny him. Their moment of choice comes to them in the Garden of Gethsemane. At some point in the drama all involved are faced with their authority to act or not. Jesus' movement to Jerusalem has a sense of destiny about it. But this does not take freedom away from the many other characters. They can be and do what they decide. The result is the cross.

Freedom, responsibility and guilt

We like to believe that having our freedom will bring us a new life and self assurance. Liberation makes a good slogan. But it is not so fine when experienced. Then freedom joins responsibility and produces guilt. When we try to act responsibly our feelings are churned up. We can never be sure that we have done everything right and feel twinges of guilt. We dislike people who seem not to feel this like us. They are too assured to be true. Normal people feel guilty. For guilt goes with freedom.

Counsellors classify guilt into two basic types. One is the guilt which comes from feeling that we have betrayed others who matter to us. It arises, for example, when we decide to break the code of behaviour in which we have been brought up. It may be as simple as the child from a teetotal family having a drink. Today's society has lax attitudes towards such things. It is "no big deal". But guilty feelings remain after we first break the rules.

But that is not the end. What we have done returns to haunt us at later moments of stress and anxiety. Many factors are at work. But the sense of failing to meet the expectations of others, especially those whom we admire, produces some guilt in all of us. Most of us live with it. It is quite normal. Only when it becomes morbid may we need treatment.

But there is another sort of guilt. This is linked to standards that we have already made our own. As we grow older we are free to make more informed choices. For example, shall we hold to a standard which our parents taught us and make it our own? Or shall we abandon it? But once we have made our decision, we stand under a new judgement if we fail to live up to it. We can no longer blame our parents. Nor can we accuse society. This is *our* standard, by which we stand or fall.

This sort of guilt cannot be treated. Indeed therapy may intensify it. No re-distribution of blame helps. It cannot be analysed: we can only seek forgiveness.

Obviously these two types of guilt cannot be completely separated. Guilt is pervasive, complex, inevitable and inexorable. It usually hits us at off moments. It is rarely a permanent state. It may also be irrational. We can feel guilty for things for which we are not directly responsible. We pass a beggar in the street. A pang of guilt shoots through us for not giving him something. We feel guilty that he exists at all. Or we watch a television programme about some distant place of which we have never heard. We are ashamed that we did not know. Guilt washes over us because we are unable to change things there. A sense of shame takes us into a complex maze of feelings. But two themes are consistently found: what it is to be responsible and our need to be forgiven.

The complex story of guilt is simply told in one of Christianity's foundation myths from the Old Testament. In the Garden of Eden the serpent invites Adam and Eve to use their freedom. It is theirs but so far they have overlooked it. Both wish to use their freedom and to discover something new about themselves, the world and their place in it. But guilt goes hand in hand with their discovery. So they hide from God. They try to lose sight of where they came from, the God who first breathed life into them. The relationship between the two of them is also altered. The whole world is affected. All the familiar complexities of our life follow.

Yet all is not misery. This process, repeated in generation after generation, makes us human. We can and still do relate to one another and to God. That is why in worship we call the Fall "the happy fault". On the day after Good Friday, awaiting Easter Day, the church's hymn, *Exsultet*, includes the line: "O happy fault, which has deserved to have such and so mighty a Redeemer."

This story does not tell us what ought to be the case. It describes our everyday life. But these days we turn it on its head. In the story the world becomes complex because Adam and Eve use their freedom. When finally they were expelled from Paradise and condemned to a harsh world, they had only each other to blame. Today, by contrast, we use the world's complexity as our excuse to disclaim responsibility. We say it is not our fault. Now that we are psychologically and sociologically informed, we blame our upbringing, environment or society. As a result we find it harder to deal with guilt. Sometimes we use these dilemmas as excuses to try to dispose of it altogether. But it does not go away.

Limited responsibility?

Young children suddenly discover the size of the world. It goes beyond all that they have known. So they try to give their full address: James Watson, 23 The Close, Somewhere, Everytown, Countryshire, England, Great Britain, Europe, The Western Hemisphere, The World, Planet Earth, The Universe and so on. With each new discovery the address becomes more complicated. The child has fun looking for limits which define where he is. Adults do the same. We are not bothered about our address. But we hunt for ways of defining ourselves in our world. In particular we need to answer this question: Where are the limits of my responsibility?

But as soon as we begin exploring, we find ourselves in a maze of unending possibilities. How much of "me" is down to my genes? How much is created by upbringing? Does housing or employment contribute to my responsibility? Just as James Watson's simple address became more complex as it was more precisely defined, so our origins seem more complicated to us. Unforeseen connections come to mind. What do we say, for example, about the industry behind the man who provided my mother with the alcohol which she unwisely drank while carrying me and so damaged my health?

Our feelings of guilt are mixed with perplexity. Our knowledge of ourselves, and new understandings of the way the world is, make us feel that we live in a world which is fixed. We are at the whim of forces which we can know or control. But in spite of this, our sense of guilt persists. It is no use being told that it is outmoded or just an illusion. People still "*know* they have played their part in the human tragedy but cannot explain exactly how."[1]

Sammy Mountjoy's dilemma

One such is Sammy Mountjoy. He appears in William Golding's novel *Free Fall*.[2] Sammy is a successful artist. But earlier in his life he exploited his first grand passion, Beatrice Ifor. He sexually degraded and, in spite of promises, deserted her. He despises himself for what he did. He knows that his behaviour was appalling. Now he cannot escape from his sense of guilt. So he rummages through his life to find the cause. Many episodes feel as though they might have added to his growing sense of guilt. But no single incident explains it.

He naturally goes back to his childhood. At school, for example, he and his friend bullied little boys and stole their cigarette cards. The head teacher told him off:

> He was a kindly, careful and conscientious man who never came within a mile of understanding his children. He let the cane stay in the corner and my guilt stay on my back. Is this the point I am looking for? No. Not here.

Sammy's life goes on. Eventually, given the type of person he has become, he convinces himself that he could not have avoided deserting Beatrice.

> I had given away my freedom. I cannot be blamed for the mechanical and helpless reaction of my nature.

When and where did he lose his freedom? Eventually he decides it was when he left school: he made a choice and fell freely. But even this discovery does not help. Sammy runs through all the people he has known in his life. But the search does not bring release or forgiveness. The answer that he comes up with is no answer. He cannot condense all his life and his mixed up behaviour into a single moment long ago. Nor can he blame his conduct with Beatrice on the influences that led to that single decision.

He has fallen and is falling – that much Sammy knows. It is happening because of a thousand and one decisions. Most of them were freely made. But all have unimaginable consequences. When any single action or series of actions seems to explain his fall, he discovers that he is more burdened than free.

Sammy Mountjoy is not unique. We all occasionally reflect on our lives to discover the moments when we abused a freedom and lost it. But because this is intensely personal, we cannot do this dispassionately. We stir up feelings. Often we can deal with them ourselves. Sometimes we turn to a counsellor or a friend for help. But still the longing for forgiveness remains.

From the first Christians have claimed that God forgives. At the beginning of the Acts of the Apostles, as the church is getting started, God's forgiveness is part of the message. The creeds later made it part of what it means to be a Christian: "I believe in the forgiveness of sins". And forgiveness is a key issue in thinking about the cross. For the Gospel includes the belief that Christ's death is God's way of forgiving our offences.

This statement can become a dogma or just a slogan.

When we allow this to happen, we diminish the importance of forgiveness, because we make pardon sound casual. But now we know, if we ever doubted it, that when people feel that they have lost their freedom and begin to feel guilty, we are dealing with deep seated emotions. No theory or statement is enough. Without an experience of release there is no forgiveness.

God's forgiveness

The way that God forgives has sometimes been presented like this: we all experience a sense of remorse; as a result we feel worthless and despair of ourselves; but from this abyss we are called to trust ourselves to God. When we do this we find a new freedom and a new start. This shows itself in a new confidence in ourselves; we become aware of our neighbour and alert to God whose service is "perfect freedom".

Like many traditional Christian schemes this one still works for some. But for Sammy Mountjoy and people like him it holds little attraction. They

> . . . need forgiveness, but they are not sure what they
> need it for. Because they cannot explain how things
> have come to happen they find it hard to open
> themselves to the good news that they have been
> forgiven . . . They cannot fit themselves into the
> general picture of having "erred and strayed like lost
> sheep".[3]

There are two reasons for this. First, we no longer instinctively feel a link between a sense of guilt and belief in God. It does not matter how strong our notion of God is. For us today guilt is more likely to be connected with ourselves and our inner world. We instinctively assume that feelings can be checked with what we know about ourselves and our motivations. So we first look inwards. Our guilt has little to do with something or someone outside us against whom we may have offended. Guilt is part of our personal make-up. Responsibility is first mine alone.

Second, our understanding of death has altered. Death is a natural process. We no longer think of it as a penalty for sin. Any idea of forgiveness, therefore, which begins with guilt, moves through sin and ends with death, does not for most people connect with what they experience.

Yet in spite of these changes, guilt remains. Pastors report that guilt is a topic on which they often counsel people. Counsellors help those for whom it has become morbid. Guilt underlies our everyday life. It emerges, for instance, in our infinite capacity for regret. "If only we had said . . .", "I wish I had just done . . . " Few of these lost opportunities are really important. But they feel significant and plague us disproportionately long after they are past.

In a world where forgiveness has become difficult, nostalgia increases. Because we are unable to heal or forget the past, we cling to all of it. Somewhere in it there is a solution to the present which we may have overlooked. One day the last piece of the jigsaw may be found and the whole puzzle completed. We look back towards a so-called "golden age". This may be when Victorian values prevailed or when everyone went to church. Each choice takes its own form. But such moments never happened. Yet because we are unable now to feel forgiven for our failings, our sense of guilt shows itself in our yearnings for a different world.

A sense of guilt and need for forgiveness is not confined to a few.

Guilt and responsibility

The Gospel addresses our sense of guilt, of whatever sort. But its message is not about removing guilt. It proclaims forgiveness. Christians also believe that God brought about this forgiveness through Christ's death. The cross, therefore, is the place to which we turn.

Christians have always disputed how God's forgiveness is achieved. Words like "expiation", "propitiation", and "mercy seat" have become slogans and sometimes weapons with which to fight. We have used them as tests of others. When I was at Oxford Archbishop Trevor Huddlestone led a university mission. One group of Christians sent him a letter asking whether he held a particular view of what God did through the cross. His reply did not use their approved language, so they did not take part. But the words we use are not in the end important. All Christians agree that God acts through the cross in some way to forgive the sins of the world.

Preachers sometimes imply that on the cross God takes responsibility for everything and everyone. All the sins and guilt of the world are gathered there. They are loaded onto the broken body and he carries them. This argument is moving. But today, as we have consistently seen, we are more aware of ourselves and our responsibility for who and what we are. So this version of the gospel is in danger of magnifying the work of God at the expense of human dignity.

Sammy Mountjoy for example, knows that whatever his

59

excuses, he cannot evade his responsibility. Every attempt to justify his behaviour leads him back to himself. So if without consulting him God takes all the wrongs of Sammy's life on himself, Sammy will not be interested. Like Sammy I feel from time to time properly guilty for what I am. I know what I have done. If God removes those feelings, he diminishes me. He may offer to release me from things for which I feel accountable. But he would do so at the expense of my self-esteem and value. Then any idea of new life, new creation, change or, in religious language, salvation, is a delusion.

The passion stories go to the heart of this dilemma. As we read and hear them, they invite us to assign blame. Who was finally responsible for Jesus' death? Whole groups may be generally accused, such as the Jews or the Romans. Or was it the result of an action by an individual such as Judas, Peter, Pilate, or Caiaphas? We search in vain for the answer. None of them alone carries the blame. Their world is precisely ours: they "*know* they have played their part in the human tragedy but cannot explain exactly how." Together they were caught up in a world beyond the grasp of any one of them.

So who does that leave? Only God himself. We find ourselves facing the inevitable: God is to blame for the crucifixion. All the people involved freely play their parts. None of the characters is a puppet and no-one is demeaned by God just using him or her. But God sets the context in which they all live out their lives. Just as in the accounts the characters of the different people are exposed for us to examine them, so is God's nature.

The cross as drama

God does not take away obligations which we instinctively know are ours. Each of the characters at the cross, for instance, is responsible for his behaviour. We judge them accordingly. The whole picture of the cross gives us the pattern of his dealings with us. God never diminishes us in order to establish his own divinity. Nor does he remove those feelings of guilt that come with our every failure to act worthily. The key lies in the fact that the cross was, and remains, public. You cannot have a private crucifixion. Humiliation and death in front of the crowd was part of the punishment. So any thinking about forgiveness which begins with the cross resists every tendency to treat guilt as private. It is never something that I have produced and with which I have to deal.

Look at two deaths from that first Good Friday: those of Jesus and Judas. Judas' suicide was private. He faced himself, perhaps was overcome with shame, and in his final exercise of freedom killed himself. His death did nothing for anyone, except possibly himself. By contrast Jesus' death was the most public available. He died for all to see and make of him whatever they wished. It was, therefore, a reference point for those around, something outside them. Through the preaching of the gospel it has remained so ever since.

When people go to a counsellor for help, they are admitting that they need someone else, in this case the counsellor, to help them break the cycle of guilt which they feel. This person becomes a reference point against which the clients can explore and re-orient their lives. Sammy Mountjoy does not go to anyone else. He believes that he

61

cannot be forgiven and the way he acts confirms this. His only reference point is himself. Every time he explores any part of his life, he gets stuck in a cycle of his own from which he cannot break out. To experience release he needs a new reference point outside himself and that cycle.

The idea of a reference point gives us a clue as to how the cross can bring forgiveness to people today. The traditional theories expect us to adopt a particular view before they can work. Take, for example, this scheme: Jesus dies in our place. We should really die because of our sin. But he accepts the consequences of our offences. This view has a long history. Some Christians still hold it today. But if no-one feels a connection between sin and death, this picture will not bring most people a sense of release or forgiveness. The picture comes from a world which is no longer ours.

Theories of the cross are unlikely today to speak to people's sense of guilt and felt need of forgiveness. If they are drawn from past eras, we cannot grasp in our experience what they are about. And our world at the moment seems too fragmented for any single way of thinking about guilt and forgiveness to be accepted. But this does not mean that the Christian message is finished. What we cannot understand, we can nevertheless feel. And the cross as a symbol and drama can still bring release.

Spectators are never passive. We take part when we watch a play. The text and the performance are not the only ingredients. Actors often comment on how an audience influences their performance. This is even true of film and television. The immediate contact between viewers and performers is broken. But the obsession with audience figures and cinema attendance reminds us that even in these more mechanical dramas the viewers contribute.

Hamlet is a play about conscience, sin and guilt. The actors come to court and Hamlet plans to use their play: "The play's the thing wherein I'll catch the conscience of the king." He continues:

> I have heard
> That guilty creatures sitting at a play
> Have by the very cunning of the scene
> Been struck to the soul that presently
> They have proclaimed their malefactions.[4]

The cross is such a drama. It has its text and its performance. Even when the theories about it decay, the story and the image can strike us anew. We may be shaken again by the starkness of the passion story itself or through representation in art or music. And in this form it is not confined to the church. The cross as symbol is found everywhere. First and foremost the cross is a spectacle, not a doctrine.

The drama of forgiveness

What then goes on at the cross that offers forgiveness? Whatever he does, God does not ask us to surrender our freedom. That is his gift to us. He made us like this and he cannot take our freedom away. We never lose responsibility for our lives, both our failures and any successes. The story of the passion is all about the characters, including Jesus himself, freely acting for better or worse. If God had relieved us of such responsibility, then the cross would not save. It could only drive us to despair. For it would remove our only secure status: that we are God's creatures.

To be forgiven is not to have what belongs to us taken away. That would be demeaning. Yet we also feel the need to be forgiven for things which we feel that we have done but which we cannot quite grasp. When God forgives he does not just release us from guilt at having offended against him. He puts all of our life – those parts with which we can deal and those which are beyond us, as Sammy found – in a new setting. In the spectacle of the cross we can watch what it means for God publicly to take responsibility for our behaviour and its consequences. Our lives and actions, even those for which we feel most guilty and have the greatest remorse, turn out to be part of the world which God has made. At the cross he publicly acknowledges this. God affirms that he is responsible for the world of which we are part. But he also offers a reference point outside ourselves by which to re-order our lives and start afresh.

Susan Howatch's novel, *Scandalous Risks*, is set in the 1960s. The new theology of Bishop John Robinson's *Honest to God* is the main talking point in the Cathedral Close at Starbridge. The Dean is in favour. The lay people are confused. The Bishop is determined to resist it. Everyone in the story has his or her secrets, their pains and distresses, as well as the joys that go with them. The Bishop drafts his chapter on ethics:

> Christianity . . . deals with people as they are – and often they're suffering, floundering amid tragedy, perhaps even screaming in agony as a result of their wrong actions and the wrong actions of others . . . When a man is being crucified during his personal Good Friday, he needs someone who symbolizes

Easter Sunday and the redemptive love of Christ, not some sunny natured fool who bounces around at the foot of the cross and showers him with sentimental goodwill.[5]

The cross always stands in the real world. There it tests how far we are willing to face the facts of God's world, especially ourselves. "The very cunning of the scene" strikes us to our souls. "Soul" means the core of our being as created, free, responsible, flawed, guilty, confused and suffering people.

The guilty people watching Hamlet's play "proclaimed their malefactions". The drama of the cross also calls us to confess. Without confession there is no forgiveness. This is not because God is mechanical. You do not put your confession in at one end of his system and take absolution out at the other. Confession links guilt and forgiveness. It does so through what we feel. Guilt is always felt. It gnaws away at us and cannot be explained away. The same is true of forgiveness. We need to feel forgiven, not only be told that we are. Confession is the outward expression of an inward feeling.

Hamlet's play moved the audience inwardly, but they responded outwardly. Confession is a public act: we do it before others, whether a priest or a congregation. Obviously we can never confess everything. Occasionally rigorist movements insist on public self-abasement by detailed disclosure. But God does not expect us to confess every detail of our lives, not least because we can never know them. We now know enough about ourselves to realize that we are like icebergs. Underneath our public behaviour there

65

is a mass of unconscious activity. When we confess we acknowledge that the way we have used our freedom has impacts on others. We know that we cannot be entirely blamed for all of these. But we also cannot escape the feeling that we are responsible for them, because we are. That is why we need forgiveness.

Forgiveness and judgement

We confess; God forgives. But where has his judgement gone? Judgement is surely part of the cross. If it is left out and we move straight from our guilt to our need for forgiveness, a crucial step is missing.

When we pass judgement on ourselves or others we confirm that there has been an offence. This is what causes Sammy's anguish. He knows that he has offended against Beatrice. Regardless of how he rationalizes what he did, he continues to feel that it was wrong. He tries to restrict the sense of offence to one person or one occasion. If he could succeed, he would still feel guilty. But at least he would identify what he has done and maybe ask forgiveness for it. He might, for instance, meet Beatrice and ask her to forgive him for having wronged her.

She might even do so. But Sammy's awesome discovery is this: his sense of offence cannot be reduced to one person or occasion. Even if he finds Beatrice, confesses his offence, asks her to forgive him and she does so, his problem is not solved. It will go on and on. Our actions are like stones thrown into a pond. They create ripples which roll unstoppably in all directions.

The effects of our behaviour on ourselves and others are highly complex. But the more we live and act, the more we add to the sum of guilt. Guilty feelings are perplexing. The more we sense that we need forgiveness for something, the more we realize that our actions have already created a new world for ourselves and for others. So whatever forgiveness may mean there can be no going back to the previous state. Once the ripples are spreading, we cannot control them or call them back.

Today we are aware of the enormous potential in the tiniest action. Chaos Theory, for example, explores the butterfly effect, "the notion that a butterfly stirring the air today in Peking can transform storm systems next month in New York".[6] Its scientific status may remain questionable. But this theory rings bells with us. People today are generally sceptical of grand schemes. We know too well how easily something which is in itself insignificant unexpectedly becomes a major importance:

> Who changes the world? Oh, this and that,
> strands as they happen to fall, tiny ligatures,
> particular here and nows, vast loopings
> of pattern, the ties and let-gos of a knot,
> small x-shapes of history; our spoor and signature
> a gauze of junctures, a nettedness of things.[7]

Judgement is about discerning how complex things are. In *Hamlet* the spectators are "struck to the soul" and "proclaim their malefactions". This describes a three stage process. First they feel guilty. The third stage is when they confess. But between these phases there is a second: they have to discover what is happening outside them that rings bells with what they feel inside. They make a judgement about themselves and their setting. In order to confess they first have to pass this judgement. It is not imposed on them by some other judge.

God has sometimes been presented as if he were such a judge. In the crucified Jesus, so the argument runs, he passed sentence on humankind and inflicted a terrible penalty upon the innocent one who took our place. There were good reasons why this idea once emerged. But for most of us it is now unbelievable. A vengeful God who harms the innocent in order to excuse the guilty is intolerable. But because we reject this picture, it does not mean that we abandon the idea of judgement.

Today we understand judgement working in two directions. We examine the setting in which we find ourselves and at the same time we assess ourselves. One without the other is not enough. So, for instance, we may consider apartheid wrong and make that judgement. We evaluate the setting. But we know in our better moments that to pass such a judgement on South Africa without judging our own behaviour is hypocritical. We know a great deal today about that self-scrutiny which leads to judgement, as well as the longing for forgiveness.

But the idea of God's judgement is not lost. We may not see him as the courtroom figure over against us. He is more part of the process of the play. Through, as it were, all the contributors to the play – author, actors, setting and so on – God's process of judgement runs. His judgement does not come from outside our world. It turns out to be, as we have seen with forgiveness and confession, in the process itself.

The uniqueness of the cross

Micheal O'Siadhail wrote about the "particular here and

nows" of our lives. How can one of these, the cross on Calvary, affect us today? A striking thing about any play is the many levels on which is operates at the same time. Once an author wrote it. In that sense, from the moment the text was produced, the play was fixed in the past. But performances can only happen now, as actors and audience combine in the theatre. However often the play is re-enacted, each performance is unique. Once it is over, it is finished. It can never be repeated. But it will have brought about some change, creating new conditions for the next show. So each performance also affects the future. It is not surprising that the great religious stories are seen as dramas or that the worlds of the theatre and of the church so frequently coincide. A drama runs through past, present and future.

The cross is God's drama. Once it happened. But now there is no moment when the production is not being presented, watched and affecting people. St Paul expresses this mixture of drama and experience in his testimony about the cross, guilt, judgement and confession and forgiveness:

> God forbid that I should be confident in anything except the cross of our Lord Jesus Christ. Through it the world is crucified to me and I to the world (Galatians 6:14).

For Paul the cross is fixed at a moment in history. But as Jesus was crucified once and for all, so Paul's experience is of his past world being crucified and set aside for ever. That is the basis on which he confidently lives. This he does here and now. Every moment of his life is present and that present is directed by being caught up in the drama of the cross. But because the world is crucified to him and he to the world, there has been a fundamental change which also alters his future.

St Paul was judged by the cross, confessed and knew that he was forgiven. But even more importantly those failures in his life for which he dimly feels responsible but which he cannot precisely identify are also forgiven. The cross has become part of him: it is the pattern of his life and he has made it his own. Yet it always stands outside him ,working on him and the world. That work is perpetual judgement, the step between his confession and knowing that he is forgiven.

St Paul's dilemma is exactly that of Sammy Mountjoy and his modern companions. They have no language in common but their experience is the same. "They *know* they have played their part in the human tragedy but cannot explain exactly how."[8] But neither Paul nor Sammy have to explain. The hope of being forgiven lies for both of them not in more self-knowledge. Each knows about guilt. And each understands self-judgement. So for both confession becomes an option.

Our freedom cannot be taken from us. That is why it is sometimes frightening. But the guilt, judgement and confession which follow from our being free can together lead to the profound release of forgiveness. God offers this in the drama of the cross, where we see what it means for him to respect the freedom which he has given us.

In 1825 Sir John Bowring published his hymn based on the text from Galatians:

> In the cross of Christ I glory,
> Tow'ring o'er the wrecks of time.

He only got it half right. There is no moment in time over which the cross towers. But there are the many "here and nows" of our lives, through which the ripples of the drama of the cross savingly run.

FOR DISCUSSION

1. Where has the sense of guilt gone in today's world? Has it disappeared, or is it disguised as something else?

2. Can we do anything for someone who feels that they cannot be forgiven?

3. Does the idea of the cross as drama make sense for you? If so, how might it today be presented?

CHAPTER 3

THE VISIT TO AUSCHWITZ

Facing Torment

Matthew 26:36–56
From Gethsemane to the Arrest

We continue with Matthew. He devotes much space to the story of Gethsemane. Two strands fit uneasily together. One is dominated by the notion of Jesus' hour (*vv.* 36, 39, 43, 45); the other by the theme of watching and testing (*vv.* 37, 38, 39b, 40, 41). **Gethsemane** means 'olive press' and may have been a garden to which Jesus and his disciples often went (John 18:1ff). The story is rich in Old Testament images: for example, falling to the ground and the cup. But the language is like that of the Lord's Prayer. The story may have been used in teaching on prayer. *V.* 45 marks the turning point: **Sleep now and rest.** After the struggle to learn what obedience means, Jesus goes confidently as God's anointed one to meet his end. The **kiss** (*v.* 49), which would have been either on the hand or the foot, was a greeting of honour. As the story progresses all means of avoiding the cross are gradually removed. The servant's **sword** (*vv.* 51ff) offers no way; nor do **twelve legions of angels** (*v.* 53). Matthew concludes by invoking the Scripture and its fulfilment (*v.* 56) and Jesus the pioneer goes alone to his death: **Then all the disciples abandoned him and fled.** (*v.* 56).

CHAPTER 3

The appalling vision
Towards the end of the nineteenth century a new order
seemed to be emerging. The world was reasonably peaceful.
Learning was advancing. Social reform proved that life did
not have to be what it always had been. Medicine was
offering new cures. Psychology and sociology were changing
the way people understood their behaviour. Religious life
and scholarship flourished. New discoveries about the
ancient world helped people come to terms with ideas about
God which they found increasingly obnoxious and difficult.
Christians were relieved to find that they could still read
the Bible. Even the primitive parts could now be kept
without too much difficulty.

Some contrasted the awesome God of the Old Testament
with a merciful Father-like God. The gospels gave us what
Jesus had taught about him. The letters of St Paul and others
had elaborated that message. But one book was obstinately
awkward. What were we to make of *The Revelation of St
John the Divine*? The extravagant imagery was magnificent.
The vision of the glorified Christ was inspiring. But could
a book so full of vengeance instead of forgiveness, division
in place of reconciliation, anger instead of mercy and wrath
in place of love be considered Christian? D. H. Lawrence
called it the Judas of the New Testament.[1]

German scholarship was highly esteemed. Some church
leaders in that country made the obvious suggestion.

Christianity, they argued, had brought many benefits. It had changed human nature. We had progressed beyond early and primitive ideas. Now everyone could sustain a Christian vision of the world. The time, therefore, had come to face the fact that *Revelation* was less than Christian. It should be removed from the Bible. In the event no formal decision, of course, was taken. That would have been difficult. But for most of this period the book was ignored.

A few years later the First World War broke out. Suddenly the fantastic world of *Revelation* reappeared, especially the four horsemen from chapter 6. Since then they have stayed with us. The white rider of war, arriving with new weapons in each generation, ranges the earth. There has been no moment in the lifetime of any person alive today when a war has not been in progress. And if enemies do not attack, the red horse of rebellion appears, its rider wielding the sword of civil war.

The third force – famine – is familiar. Its black horse remains as powerful as ever. Starvation is a tragedy. But for most of history it has been part of the cycle of enough and nothing. Now the media expose to us the permanent imbalance of the world. A few have too much; most have nothing. And in spite of all our efforts we cannot get the balance right.

The final horseman is disease and death. A short while ago the universal conquest of disease was thought possible. The last case of smallpox was diagnosed. Given time, it was believed, there was no reason why all epidemics should not be relegated to the past. But then there appeared the first signs of AIDS. Death reasserted its power to strike unpredictably.

77

Far from being a curiosity of history *Revelation* still provides the sort of imagery that we need. Our experience is so fantastic that we need this sort of visionary language to describe it. It helps us to say the unspeakable.

From suffering to torment

Most of us can just about find words to talk about personal suffering. We may use everyday language such as "pain" or "bereavement". Many add the psychological jargon of "loss", "dislocation" or "disarray". None of them are adequate when we actually experience suffering. On the whole, however, they are good enough to get us through most crises. They let us share with others something of our sorrow and even anguish.

Yet at one point they all fail. Today no one can mention suffering without going beyond their own experience. The persistent enigmas of war, civil strife, famine and pestilence are inescapable. Individuals sometimes suffer terrible personal anguish. But we feel this in the context of even greater agony.

In this century millions have not only seen visions of hell: they have lived there. Many still do. The word "suffering" is not enough. It covers too much and says too little. What is the connection between my suffering and that of the millions of whom I hear? No one can judge, least of all me. We could never say that one is more important than the other. But if both are "suffering", what sort of comparison are we being invited to make?

It is better to find different words. Leave "suffering" to our personal experiences. Suffering is usually passive. It generally happens to us. "Torment" is a better word to describe the large-scale agonies of our world. Behind it lies a stronger sense of intention. The place of everlasting torment is called "hell". Torment and hell remind us that people do terrible things to one another.

Suffering disturbs. But it is often possible to see how something better might follow. Mother was plaiting the little girl's hair. It pulled a little and she cried out. "There's no beauty without pain," said mother. The Greeks made a motto of the same idea: "Suffering teaches". Some versions of Christianity endorse this idea. Through Christ's suffering, the argument goes, mankind is redeemed. Suffering is no longer just something that happens to us. It can bring about some positive good.

This scheme once worked even in the face of torment. Evil could be regarded as the work of evil powers. But Christ had conquered these. The mighty theme of Christ triumphing over the principalities and powers of this world has a long history. Earlier in this century some teachers predicted that its time would soon come again. And in a sense it has.

The victory of a mighty leader over powerful forces ranged against him is one of today's popular myths. Films portray bold but erratic policemen, who single-handed clean up corrupt cities. Superman and Batman overcome wrongdoers. Obe ben Kenobi and Luke Starwalker defeat Darth Vader in *Star Wars*. They have even given us a new blessing – "May the force be with you".

This theme is attractive. It feeds our hope that a magical intervention might save us. But once a gulf grows between such suffering as I know and the world's torment, which is beyond my experience, so simple a solution rings increasingly false. Life is not like that. A divine rescuer is scarcely more credible than Superman. And even if he rescues me, what about all those others? There is some truth in these pictures. But as a way seriously to help us face the horror of torment in our world such a scheme no longer works.

Death revalued

One reason is that death is not what it was. We have already seen that Christian thought used to connect death with sin. Because we failed to remain in God's image, the argument ran, death entered the world. It can only be defeated as sin is overcome. On our journey from birth to death we all suffer. But, we are told, the experience, properly used, can be spiritually improving. In particular suffering can prepare us for a good death. After that we shall be reunited with God. And if we end up insufficiently purified by suffering in this life, then purgatory might cover the point.

This approach is not bankrupt. It remains one way of meditating on two certainties in life: personal suffering and death. We might, like St Francis, gracefully welcome death as a sister or, with Dylan Thomas, "Rage at the dying of the light".[2] People have always held a range of attitudes between these extremes.

But in this century everything has changed. We no longer have to contend only with our own death and those of people we know. Every one of us also knows about the millions of victims who die because of war, pestilence and famine. We have learned that all of us are not so much mortal as vulnerable. Like those millions we feel that we too will be death's victims.

Death today no longer naturally links with suffering. It goes hand in hand with evil. The sum of its victims overwhelms us. For instance, casualties in this century's two world wars are countless. In the 1914–18 war generals planned for thousands of soldiers to die. By 1939–45 civilians had taken their place. Since then the figures seem only to get worse.

Awesome as the numbers are, even they fade before one specific torment in our western, Christian culture: Auschwitz-Birkenau. There were other camps. But here death consumed one human being per minute, day and night, for three years. More Jews were murdered here than anywhere else. Auschwitz stands as the symbol of the horror that is now usually called "The Holocaust".

If we try hestitatingly to ask what, if anything, Auschwitz means, we discover why the question of suffering has been transformed into that of torment. However we look at Auschwitz, it speaks of the purposeful extermination of whole peoples and takes us to the edge of any human evil that we can conceive. Can religious people any more speak of God after this? If we dare to, we now have no choice: we must do so with Auschwitz and the torment which it stands for in mind.

Auschwitz the place of torment

"Auschwitz" symbolizes the slaughter of six million Jews and five million others, one and a half million of them children. This horror cannot be explained. But it was brought about by a mix of political aims, religious power and sheer brutish inhumanity. The result was the torment of the innocent.

Christians use the same words about the crucifixion. There, too, politics, religion and inhuman viciousness led to innocent suffering. We also claim that Jesus' death was a unique instance of God at work. But Auschwitz forces parallels on us. Until now we were at least sure that the cross was unique. Now its uniqueness is itself questioned.

To enter the swirling dilemmas raised by Auschwitz and all that it stands for, we need a few fixed points. Otherwise we will be overwhelmed and unable to think or pray. One such marker is a statement of faith: however impossible it seems and however much our faith is stressed, we can never separate God from torment.

We often link the cross with the world's torment. But before we can make such a connection we must first feel the shock of that torment. Christians will wish to claim that Christ's cross was as much in Auschwitz as anywhere in the world. But the cross does not illuminate torment and help us to see it for what it is. Torment is torment, whether we invoke the cross or not. In fact the cross challenges every temptation to make casual connections between God, torment, Auschwitz, Christ and the cross.

After the Holocaust a Jewish woman, catching sight of a huge cross displayed in New York City each year at Christmastime, said to her walking companion, Father Edward H. Flannery, "That cross makes me shudder. It is like an evil presence." Although the cross had already been the dread symbol of murdering crusaders, inquisitors, and pogromists, in and through the *Endlösung* [The Final Solution], it became ultimately corrupted by devilishness.[3]

For Christians the cross is a good thing. We have prettified it as an ornament. Some believe that it might ward off evil. The hymns and prayers of centuries have made it seem manageable. We speak casually, make the sign of the cross unthinkingly, and slickly resolve its contradictions with our doctrines. But still it returns to test us. If in our generation we are in danger of becoming insensitive to the cross, God stirs us through Auschwitz.

All the themes of that one cross on which one Jew died are thrust back to us from Auschwitz where so many Jews were killed. Crucifixion was not a Jewish form of punishment. It was Roman. But all three men who died on Good Friday were Jews. The cross has become the supreme Christian symbol. So we assume that it belongs to us. But it can never be ours alone. Like the crucifixion on that first Good Friday Auschwitz was a place of "The Final Solution".

It is more than a matter of interest or religious courtesy that Christian reflection on Christ's cross should take into account Jewish responses to Auschwitz. It is one way of re-discovering what we ourselves believe.

God and the cross after Auschwitz

For Jewish thinkers Auschwitz does not stand for a past event. The treatment of the Jews and other sufferers there is so unique that they cannot even agree on a word to describe it. Whatever we call it, what happened at Auschwitz is chiefly found in the stories that are still told about it. Some are factual, some fictional, some documented and some passed on by word of mouth. Auschwitz remains an experience. It is not just what the victims felt in the past. Auschwitz is still felt in the present.

Because of this no one can just discuss the Final Solution. Once we know about it, we have to reach a conclusion. Jewish thinkers note that this is particularly true for them. The popular word "holocaust" means "whole burning". The term is usually used of the sacrifice of a burnt offering to God. So as soon as we even use this word, the question arises of where God is in such torment.

Looking back to it, we can see in the Holocaust an inevitable climax to centuries of anti-semitism. It has also become a reference point for our questions about God, humanity, belief, unbelief, good and evil. It will probably not carry all these for ever. But it does for our time.

Jews display as much disagreement over the Holocaust as Christians do about the Atonement. As they died at Treblinka, Rabbi Israel Shapiro told his people that still true to God's historic call they were atoning for the sins of all mankind. Another hopeful view was that in the camps God put his covenant with his people to its final test. God proved faithful; the covenant remains in place.

Quite opposite is the thought that God is dead. Whoever he was before Auschwitz, after it God ceased to exist. God's covenant with his people places all the sorrows of Jewish history within a divine plan. But you can only tolerate so much. Any God who wills the death of six million Jews is morally insupportable.

Others simply give up. Auschwitz is part of God's inscrutable and unknowable plan. You may or may not choose to believe in it.

No Christian can choose between these ways of seeing the Holocaust. It would be presumptuous. But we cannot ignore these Jewish inquiries into God and torment. They are struggling in the context of Auschwitz with an issue that affects us all: God and torment. Yet for all their variety, these approaches have two points in common. First, they raise the question of torment, evil, God and atonement in a way and on a scale which no one can ignore. Second, the conclusions have only been reached through a struggle with God. Together these points strip away religious fripperies. They place belief in God for our age firmly where for many it belongs – on the brink of atheism.

There may be no God. Or the God in whom we believe may be false. He may even be a demon. There are limits to how many of the world's horrors we can accept as our responsibility. Some belong to God alone. But when we lay responsibility for the world's painful absurdity at the Creator's feet, he begins to look malign. Or he may just be indifferent. A distant God attracts some people by his remoteness. Others still cling to a more personal God. But he, too, in the context of torment looks increasingly powerless. We have problems. In each case he becomes no God.

The dilemma is an old one. Epicurus, a Greek philosopher who lived three hundred years before Christ, put it this way:

Is God willing to prevent evil, but not able? Then he is impotent. Is he able but not willing? Then he is malevolent. Is he both able and willing? Whence this evil?

But today there is a new factor to consider. Since Epicurus taught, Christ has come. Thinking, at least in the West, has been transformed through over 2000 more years of human experience. Have we come full circle because of torment, from the atheism of Epicurus to that demanded after Auschwitz?

Torment and belief

All of us now live on the brink of atheism. There is little room for agnosticism, the claim that "I don't know". Torment squeezes the luxury of that position. Life is too severe. We also know more about our own behaviour. We have, for example, discovered how easily any of us can inflict suffering.

Stanley Milgram devised a famous experiment. He invited people to come to his laboratory to help his research. They were told that the aim was to discover the effect of pain on learning. The experiment required them to inflict progressively stronger electric shocks on volunteers. Full power could kill, but there was no real risk of going that far. The invitees did not know it, but they were in fact the objects of the experiment. The "agonized volunteers" were actors. In the end over sixty per cent of the assistants administered maximum voltage to the volunteers, who passed out.

Whatever else the Milgram experiment shows, it illustrates how difficult we now find it to leave anything unknown. The invited assistants were willing to go to any lengths. They justified their actions to themselves. It was all right, they said, because they were involved in a scientific experiment. This was not torture: it was learning. They were helping the professor.

Like them, we believe that in principle we can find out about everything. Not to know something has itself become a problem. Which of us dares confess that we do not know?

So we find the humility of agnosticism, of admitting that we do not know something, more difficult than our predecessors.

Torment forces us to extremes. At one end is our modern arrogance: "We are the gods now". At the other honesty, itself a religious virtue, seems to demand that we admit that there may be no God. So whichever route we take, we come to the same place – the brink of atheism. God has gone; mankind, his replacement, has also failed. Auschwitz stands for both possibilities.

Christians sometimes invoke Christ's cross in response to this dilemma. But the answers become trite. They are even reduced to slogans: "Trust God"; "Obey Jesus"; "Have faith". But we already know that they do not work. The most famous slogan in the New Testament was nailed to the cross: "Jesus of Nazareth, the King of the Jews". It was written by Pilate, had to be in three languages to be understood and was disputed as soon as it was posted. Making things simple brought its own problems.

Complexity is not necessarily a bad thing. The writer to the Ephesians speaks about God's "intricately varied wisdom" (Ephesians 3:10). Only with some such sense of depth can we face the profound question of torment.

The cross, suffering and torment
Since New Testament times Christians have been notable for the way that they bear suffering. They may become stoic: "We all have our cross to bear". Some make this an excuse for apathy. But others endure suffering nobly and impressively. Their courage adorns the faith and is a human glory.

The danger is that those who can steel themselves to bear this burden may become less than Christian. They bear their self-determined cross on their own terms. And they make others suffer because of it. But in the end the cross tests such stoicism and rejects it. It is not the Christian way. Dying on a cross can never be thought of as heroic.

The stoic suffers majestically but alone. But Christ's suffering on the cross was certainly not private. In the Berkeley Chapel at Bristol Cathedral you can just see fading wall paintings either side of the altar. Each is the outline of a crucified figure. They need the third. He was on the altar between them, as either a crucifix or the bread and wine. These paintings are a rare instance of the two crucified bandits being remembered at the heart of Christian worship. Artists bring the three together in their paintings. But worshippers concentrate on Jesus and usually forget the other two.

In the passion story the two thieves remind us that there is always more than one cross. Jesus was not crucified alone. That day he was one of three; historically one of millions. He was not in that sense unique. His cross is always tied to the suffering of others.

Suffering does not just have to be quietly endured. This is especially true of torment. Should it happen to me, I hope that I might be able calmly to face terrible news about myself. We are rightly impressed, for example, when someone bears terminal cancer with fortitude. Some even manage it with a kind of gaiety. They are not quietly passive. Nor do they just endure. Their liveliness comes about because they make connections between their suffering and the world outside them. They do not allow themselves to become isolated in their pain.

These people make their anguish active and creative because they deliberately do not turn in on themselves. The courageous woman dying of cancer, for example, expands the range of her relationships during the time she has left. Some use their illness to bring hope to others. They form associations or raise money. The forgiving Ulsterman refuses to avenge his daughter's murder. He joins himself and his sadness to the disrupted lives of others. He, his dead daughter, her murderers, and even we who learn about the episode, are brought together.

Instances like these create unsuspected connections between people. They draw the rest of us into the close circle of those involved. Our lives are changed, too. Bearing suffering is far more than stoic endurance or passive acceptance. It is an active way of living.

But this approach, impressive as it is, will not do in the face of torment. The agonies of others, especially the innocent, demand protest. The Jewish scholar, Emil Fackenheim, shows us what resistance might mean. Since Auschwitz, he argues, there is a new commandment: the true Jew is forbidden to give Hitler another, posthumous victory. Anyone giving up their faith would be doing just that. It would mean that a Jew would become a non-Jew and hence no more than another dead Jew. Therefore, Jews are commanded

to survive as Jews, lest the Jewish people perish, . . .
to remember in our very guts and bones the martyrs of the Holocaust, lest their memory perish. [Jews] are forbidden . . . to deny or despair of God . . . lest Judaism perish, [and] to despair of the world . . . lest

89

we make everything a meaningless place in which God is dead or irrelevant and everything is permitted.[5]

This protest is not a cry of righteous indignation. It offers a way to live, because so many died. The stance is very near that of the cross.

At first glance Jesus, who "was led like a lamb to the slaughter and was dumb before the shearers", seems to stand against any idea of protest. The text is from Isaiah 53, a Song of the Suffering Servant. The chapter seems uncannily to describe what happened at the crucifixion. It has become a favourite of many Christians, although the earliest Christians hardly referred to it.

The passage emphasizes silence in the face of attack. To us that looks like a way of avoiding protest. We are used to people speaking out, often loudly, and making their voice and message heard. Jesus' silence leaves us uncomfortable. But the first Christians did not use it as an excuse to avoid protest. The issue for them was: On whose behalf was Jesus silent? Was it himself? Or was it for another reason?

When we do something on behalf of someone else a transaction is involved. Transaction is a persistent theme in thinking about the cross. We may accept that we will never understand what goes on there. But we feel that on the cross God deals with something. There he transacts business of some sort. But if he does, he must do something about the continuing torment in his world. If he avoids this, then God is absent from a major part of his world, as we know it. And if that were true, atheism would be our only option. So from the brink of atheism we demand, if there is a God, to know what he is doing.

Torment is part of the larger problem of evil. The cross itself illustrates this. Crucifixion was a torment. It involved deliberate and extraordinary cruelty. But even the ancients, who lived in a much harsher world than ours, called it evil. Auschwitz is like that for our age. Through it, too, we learn about torment and are overwhelmed with the scale of evil.

In order to face evil we often focus it in a supremely evil person or group. Judas was once useful for this. Sadly Christians have sometimes treated the Jews in the same way. In this century Hitler, Stalin and Saddam Hussein have each served their turn. Coming to Auschwitz, however, we discover again what in our heart of hearts we already knew. Of course evil people exist. But however evil we think any one person is, he or she does not explain evil. It occurs on such a scale that it even swamps what we mean by "person".

Christianity has connected evil with the Devil. We like to see the world in terms of a battle: the Devil versus God. In practice evil seems to win. The Devil then emerges as more attractive, competent and powerful. And as this evil becomes more prominent we begin to lose touch with the reality of God.

A passage in Isaiah 59 illuminates what happens to us. It is especially useful since the writer did not escape the problem by talking of a devil. He does not have our way of simplifying things. But like us he knew how despair distorts our thinking. He dwells on how hopeless our human situation is. Evil dominates and no-one seems able to do anything about it:

We look for light, but all is darkness; we look for brightness, but walk in deep shadow ... Truth is nowhere to be found; and whoever resists evil becomes its prey.

We are stuck. We are only going to be able to move if something breaks in from outside us. That is what happens:

God saw that there was no one to intervene; he was appalled. So with his own arm he worked his salvation.

This is our experience. The monumental evil of torment, belief in God and the idea of the Devil make a powerful mix. But together they call for action. Someone somehow has to do something.

This felt pressure produced a way of thinking about God, torment and evil that was once powerful. In the cross, the story ran, we watch a transaction between God and the Devil. They do business together for ownership of the world or our souls. For most of us now the picture is unbelievable. We do not escape the problem of torment by turning it into a struggle between good and evil or God and the Devil. This is the theology of Westerns. The good guy and the bad guy shoot it out. One wins, the other loses. In real life, however, we know that good and evil are more complicated.

But the dilemma that such pictures represent is still with us. If we abandon the Devil, evil does not go away. Our world is full of malign forces. Auschwitz did happen. Torment continues. We may not be able to explain all this. But we do need to be able to speak about it. To do that we must have images.

People who believe in God live with the fact of evil as much as everyone else. So however difficult it may seem, we must hold God and evil together. Jews have found that they can do this without a devil. But they still have their symbols of evil. Today's is Auschwitz. They say, for instance, either we must abandon our usual ways of thinking about God or we have to believe that every moment of evil is one when God in some way reveals himself.

There is no alternative for religious people. For Christians the point is clear. We cannot confine God's dealings with evil to a transaction between him and another being, whether the devil or a person whom we judge evil. But if we do not blame evil on the devil or a corrupt person, who is left? Once again, as we found in the last chapter, there is only God.

The evil of the cross is an instance, Christians would say the supreme instance, of God's dealings with the world he has made. There is a transaction on the cross, but not between God and something other than him. It takes place between the creator and his creation, which is this world with its pain, suffering, evil, and death. We shall later explore what this means for God himself. But for the moment, as we stand before Auschwitz and the torment it represents, we learn that we can never separate the difficult parts of our human experience and its insoluble problems from God.

To say that the transaction of the cross is between God and what he has made is not as strange as it may sound. Jesus dies on the cross and God is not successful in any way that we can prove. Even if we invoke the idea of the Devil, interpretations on this line do not help. The Devil still seems to be winning. God appears passive. Why does he not fight

– and win? Believers are human; we long like anyone else to be on a winning side.

But God's achievement lies elsewhere. Through the cross he publicly proclaims that he is responsible for every aspect of the world which he has created. Torment is endemic to God's world. He acknowledges that. He offers no defence of himself or justification for his world. The cross is, as it were, God's confession.

But just as we saw in the last chapter that confession is the first step to new hope, so now we can begin to grasp the hope that God's work on the cross brings to a tormented world. We do not have to people the world with evil beings, human or spiritual, to cope with its anguish. Torment is real and is faced as such. But because God acknowledges his place in it, this destructive force can be faced by any, including us, with both realism and hope.

The final solution

Hitler and the Nazis called the planned extermination of the Jews "The Final Solution". Christians use similar phrases about the cross. There God's aims were finally achieved: "God was in Christ, reconciling the world to himself" (2 Corinthians 5:19). We believe that the cross is our assurance that God provides a final solution even for the evils of his world. Auschwitz examines that claim.

"Final" means "last". It also means "once and for all". Christ's cross certainly happened at one time and in a specific place. But in what sense can it be God's final, once for all, act or word? Evil persists. Whatever God achieved on the cross he has not removed torment from the world. Neither was Auschwitz the last moment of human misery. Both have become symbols of continuing anguish. Auschwitz even added the word "genocide", murder of a people, to the world's vocabulary.

Some try to get around the problem of continuing evil by arguing that for the saved evil is not real. Because Christ died they are free from its shackles. It no longer affects them. But this is an exclusive use of the cross. It implies that it benefits a few only. Whenever we may be tempted to follow that track, the story prevents us. The cross has no redeeming features. It is unquestionably evil. And it links a host of people, disciples, the crowd, priests, Judas, Pilate, Herod and so on, in ways that they did not expect. But not one is unaffected by its evil. All are contaminated. No one is "saved".

Others even suggest that there is no such thing as evil. What we call "evil" is the sum of people's behaviour. If people would behave better, evil would cease. But we know from our experience that opportunities for wrongdoing disturbingly coincide with our willingness to take them. The Nazis' attempt to exterminate the Jews, for instance, might be put down to German culture, to Hitler's beliefs and to the behaviour of individuals. No one can evade being accountable by claiming that they were obeying orders. There is a bit of truth in that defence. But evil is always more than the sum of actions by individuals.

So we must think again. "Final" can mean "ultimate" as well as "the last". In this sense it refers to quality. Obviously no final act of God can be his last action with us. Otherwise he could not be doing anything with us now. But a particular act, like the cross, fixed in time and place, can be his ultimate dealing. In it lies all God has to give on the subject of torment. It is inexhaustibly rich and the only limit to it is how much we can receive. In this sense "final" is not confined to its past or present effects. It includes what God is also going to do in the future.

God's final act in the cross stands as a dead-end. We cannot get behind it in order to put our world straight. There may be some reasons why it occurred. But no explanation alters its starkness. The same is true of Auschwitz. Millions of words have been written, ideas conceived and explanations offered. But when all has been said and written, both Auschwitz and Calvary remain. They are in this sense ultimate, final instances of torment.

We have seen that going back to find the causes of things does not bring hope. Yet we seem to be made to wonder how things came to be and why they are as they are. For many aspects of our life this is good enough. But torment is different. We face it, knowing that nothing could adequately explain it. Yet we still long to know why it happens. We cannot escape this dilemma, any more than we can avoid torment. But the cross offers us a way to live with the problem.

The cross is never solely a past event. At one moment in history Jesus was crucified on Golgotha. From that moment his death has never been forgotten. But it is not simply remembered. Daily it is brought into the present as people hear the story in word and watch it again proclaimed in the sacrament. So we never go back to the cross. Rather, it is constantly brought into our present. It is, therefore, always here and now. It stands for God's continuing work, his transaction between himself and the world he has made, including its torment. No part of that, whatever the problems, is outside his actions.

96

No Christian, therefore, can ever be casual about suffering and torment. Nor does the Gospel offer an answer to them. But the cross is not only the one on which Jesus died. It is also what each person is invited to carry. For many it will be the cross of personal suffering. For all, if we look carefully, it will be the cross of the world's torment. No sensitive person can be immune to that. And all must feel helpless before it. But since this is also God's cross, no-one ever carries alone whatever cross happens at the moment to be theirs, whether a private one of suffering or the public one of evil and torment. The cross does not take away the pain of suffering or explain the agonies of torment. But it does give hope to us as we live with both.

"One ever hangs"

The fact of torment offers believers a stark choice. Either there is no God at all; or, if we are still driven to faith, we have to believe in a God who is inescapably caught up in torment. We do not have the luxury of indifference.

We admire the active heroes of the faith. Their names are the roll-call of the saints. In Hebrews 11 the writer lists men and women whose faith was vigorous. All, named and nameless, did something. He exhorts us to follow them. But he bases this call on Christ's cross. It provides the style for every disciple of the crucified. Like a lode the cross runs through all aspects of human life. Whether in massive events like Auschwitz or the smallnesses of our lives, the cross is God's final statement on torment and suffering. It stands for God's action in dealing with them. So in every aspect of our lives we, too, have to come to our decisions and act.

We may not consider ourselves heroic. But when the cross

is held before us we realize that it is not valiant to be crucified. There is not much bravery in the passion stories. The decisions of those involved, including Jesus, are very ordinary. The most confident is "Arise! Let us go forward". Jesus goes to meet the trial, condemnation and the cross. But the decision is only taken after the struggles with uncertainty in Gethsemane. Amid the torment of the world the cross offers us this message: we, too, may have to take a similar stand.

The cross tests any indifference we may feel about torment. It particularly judges us when we turn away from the torment of others. Jesus was not the only person in history who was unkindly betrayed, unfairly tried, unjustly condemned and miserably crucified. He represents millions. And, says the gospel, this crucified Jew is God's final, or ultimate, word on torment.

Early in this century, long before Auschwitz, soldiers experienced previously unimaginable anguish in the trenches of Flanders. Sensitive men found their trust in one another and faith in God stretched beyond endurance. Among these was Wilfred Owen. Passing along the roads of France and Belgium he saw little Calvaries, models of the crucifixion. Some were still standing; some were destroyed; many were askew because of the shelling. But through it all, whatever the torment, a sense of Christ's continuing suffering remained.

> One ever hangs where shelled roads part.
> In this war too he lost a limb.
> But his disciples hide apart;
> And now the soldiers bear with him.[6]

Amid the cynicism of despair at the agonies of this world and the simplistic excuses of his disciples, he still hangs. The effects of his cross continue. Because of that it is God's final solution. But unlike the Final Solution of Auschwitz, it is not something that he does to others. This final solution is more awesome, because this torment is what God allows to happen to him.

FOR DISCUSSION

1. Think of examples of torment today. What does the Christian gospel have to say about them?

2. Do you see realistic signs of hope in a tormented world? What should the church (at any level of its life) be doing about them?

3. In what ways can you now understand Christ's offering of himself "once and for all"? How important is this theme to Christian faith?

CHAPTER 4

DUD AND PETE'S PHILOSOPHY

The Limitations of Power

Luke 23:26–48
From Condemnation to Crucifixion

Luke, like Matthew, has his own view of the crucifixion. For him Jesus is a righteous prophet, so he has to suffer. Luke has a strong sense of destiny. This might be something to do with his having Greeks and Romans in mind rather than Jews. They would have been more familiar with the idea of fate. According to Luke Jesus' mission was to save the lost. So he dies between two bandits. Jesus serves to the end and in his final words, **into your hands I commend my spirit,** manages himself in a way that Matthew, Mark and John do not recognize. Jesus' final journey begins with a model of discipleship: **Simon of Cyrene** carries the cross **behind Jesus** (v. 26). The terrors (vv. 28–31) probably refer by the time of this Gospel to the Fall of Jerusalem in 70 A.D. The **criminals** (v. 32) are Jesus' companions, his new disciples, throughout. **Father, forgive them** (v. 34) contrasts with what crucified men were expected to say. They usually confessed their guilt or cursed their enemies. The offering of vinegar (v. 36) is another mockery. Luke alone gives words to the criminals. **Remember us** (v. 42) is a formula derived from memorial inscriptions. Jesus' response **Today you will be with me in Paradise** (v. 43) is less about life after death than about the promise of life here and now, even on the point of death. The portents in vv. 44ff are actually impossible. But Luke is drawing on a long tradition of imaginative writing. At Jesus' birth the light of the star and the angels turned night into day. At his death day becomes

103

night. The symbols continue with the tearing of the curtain, the confession of the centurion and the effect of Jesus' death on the crowd and his followers. Luke mixes fantastic symbols with Jesus' concern for the people involved in the cross. The signs indicate who dies; the loving behaviour of Jesus and others demonstrates God's love for all humankind.

CHAPTER 4

Peter Cook and Dudley Moore created two memorable down and outs called Dud and Pete. Dud was the inquirer; Pete the expert. Each week they discussed the ultimate questions of the universe – why are things as they are? Once they examined the problem of God. The topic was obviously important. But was there any proof that he existed? Finally they agreed that God needed to burst through the clouds and appear in a blaze of golden light. No great message was required. He only had to say, "Yoo, hoo! Here I am. Believe in me." But, they concluded, since he did not do this, we can go no further on the question.

Devout Christians say that they do not want any such proof. Belief in God is a matter of faith. They might also claim that God has revealed himself in Jesus Christ. But both answers are in a sense a cop out. And for many people, believers included, Pete and Dud's question persists. Behind it lies the question of power. What, if there is a God, is he (or she) capable of? If there is a God, why does he seem to do so little? What is it to speak of God, if we do not think of power.

The quest for power
We pray to "Almighty God". Popular modern hymns emphasize triumph – "Our God reigns!" The words stress that by "God" we mean someone who is totally powerful. In recent years there has been a decline in public religion.

This has made the question of God more, not less, acute. Christian responses divide roughly into two. One is to search eagerly for evidence of God's power. The other is to try to justify his weakness.

Concern with power, who has it and who can use it, marks much modern religion. Authoritarian forms of Islam are re-emerging in its traditional strongholds as well as in the West. If believers distance themselves from the corrupting influences of the West, God's power will again be released. In India and Pakistan Sikhism, Hinduism, Buddhism, Christianity and Islam are all zealous to prove their strength. In the Middle East Judaism and Islam are in conflict over the same problem.

For Western Christianity, for example, the mass media are seductive. Billy Graham wrote:

> Television is the most powerful tool of communication ever devised by man . . . in a single telecast I preach to millions more than Christ did in his lifetime.[1]

Robert Schuller's popular television programme is called *The Hour of Power*. Not only in America people believe that such powerful means of communication must be claimed by the church to spread its gospel. Then the power of God will be reasserted in a world which is hostile to him.

The Holy Spirit is also linked with power. Spirit-filled churches are eager to claim the power of God's spirit working among their people. Tongues, healings and dramatic conversions all witness to it.

Power is also a central issue for some of the newly emerging post-Christian religions, for example, the range of beliefs within the New Age. Astrology is about what sort of control the stars and planets have over our destinies. It offers us the chance of manipulating that power. Or the psychology of human potential may release within us powers which we have overlooked. Nature's forces might be harnessed through crystals and pyramids, or by returning to pagan beliefs.

Wherever we look concern with power dominates: Where is it to be found? How can we join it? Can we turn it to our benefit? Is surrender to some external power our only option? Power and control go together. Powerlessness means a loss of control, having things taken out of our hands when we ought to be able to do better.

The alternative to this concern with God's power is belief in God who seems to be increasingly weak. He is pushed to the edges of life. The full-blooded God of the Jewish and Christian tradition fades. He looks dangerously like the Cheshire Cat:

> It vanished, quite slowly, beginning with the end of the tail, and ending with the grin which remained some time after the rest of it had gone.[2]

About the same time as Dud and Pete were philosophizing, a theological movement went under the slogan "God is dead". It was not confined to the universities. The press discussed it widely. The phrase came from Friedrich Nietzsche's parable of the lunatic. In the early morning light the madman rushed through the market place with a lantern looking for God. "Where has God gone to?" he cried, "I will tell you: we have killed him." The story was often repeated in the 1960s. We do not hear it so much today.

But the lunatic's question is still with us.

The answers to it offer us a simple choice. Either we can return to a more primitive understanding of a powerful God, as if there had been no changes in the way we understand ourselves or our world. Faith in one who can be explored is not invited. Or we may find ourselves stuck with a God who daily seems to become weaker, unable to influence either the world or us.

Both approaches – seeking power and stressing weakness – suffer from the same delusion. Each invites us to make God in our own image. We might wish him to be powerful. Then we might hope to get him to exercise that power. Or maybe we prefer a God whose interest in his creation is limited. He is not able to do anything about it. He stands by and watches.

Either way, there are problems. A God whom we can manipulate is in the end unbelievable. Who is in charge? Which of us is God? A God who is omnipotent can be admired. We would stand in awe and might even worship him. But can we ever love him? A powerless God might invite us to love him for his weakness and vulnerability. But could such a one be worshipped for long?

Four groups around the cross

A crucifixion was meant to be a spectacle. The victim was tied or nailed to the beam on the ground. It was then hoisted into the upright position so all could watch. People watched and were warned. The gospel stories tell us about four groups of spectators. Each was there for a reason. But each also represents us in our questioning about God.

First there was the crowd as a whole. It was festival time

in Jerusalem. These people had milled around the city. They had come for a party. An extra attraction was on offer. This was not the crucifixion itself. For most Jews a cross was abhorrent, not enticing. But things this year were different from usual. A strange man from the north was one of the victims. Jesus had upset the authorities and scored some points off them. In the end, however, he was having to pay the penalty. But rumour had it that he could heal and perform miracles. Some had even said that he could raise the dead – at least outside Jerusalem.

Miracles are always fascinating. Many in the crowd would, like Dud and Pete, have claimed that they would believe in God if he would do one miracle. Jesus was reported to have disturbed religious people, upset political leaders, healed the sick and raised the dead. There was a chance that he might perform the most dazzling miracle of all and cheat the cross. It was worth a look. This crowd would have been large.

Among the crowd there would have been a separate group. In any gathering there are those who are half caught up in events and half distance themselves from them. They are not indecisive, but their belief switches around. At times they go along with the crowd. A miracle might convince them of the rightness of their belief. Then they would be free from uncertainty. But another voice within reminded them that miracles prove nothing. Yet the longing remained. These people are the half-believers. They were searching for some evidence that would transform their half-belief into full commitment. They hoped to shift their little belief at least into half-belief. If asked they would never admit this. They appear aloof and quizzical, half expecting but not really believing. They hang around the edge of things.

The third group at the cross remains a mystery. The stories are tantalizingly full of hints about people of whom we know almost nothing. What, for instance, happened to all the people Jesus met in Galilee? A rich young ruler asked about eternal life and went away sadly. Zacchaeus, the tax collector, learned about forgiveness and restitution. A Syrophoenician woman bandied riddles with Jesus. What of those who were healed and did nothing? What did those who heard the sermons do with their new learning?

They were not among the first rank of disciples. But they had noticed that there was something important about Jesus. Some of them directly experienced his effect on them. We can imagine them on that Friday standing around the cross, looking for some assurance that their expectations had not been misplaced. They were religious people. As Jesus' death loomed they became increasingly disappointed. But they would not give up. They stood there hoping for something to happen.

And finally there were the chosen disciples. By now almost all had fled. The disciples left at the cross are mostly the women. They had cared for Jesus and his men on the road. For the sake of the Kingdom of God they had put themselves out. Now it looked ominously as though it might have been for nothing. So they stood there, watching and praying for God to prove Jesus right. Then they could finally be sure about their decision to believe, trust, follow and act.

In 1966 the Swiss New Testament scholar, Eduard Schweizer, was invited to lecture in Japan. He could not take many books with him. But on the journey he wrote a book, *Jesus*. It contains the distilled wisdom of a lifetime's study of the New Testament. This is how he reflects on the crucifixion:

> "Let Christ the king of Israel come down from the cross that we may see and believe" (Mark 15:32), they shout. And they kept on shouting, while he perished in misery. And the miracle, boldly demanded, secretly expected, devoutly hoped for, and ardently prayed for, did not take place.[3]

Here are our four groups: the crowd boldly demanding a miracle; the half-believers secretly expecting it; the religious people devoutly hoping for it, and the disciples ardently praying that it might happen. Each group had different expectations. But underneath these each shared the same hope and prayer: if only God would do something.

We can find what these groups stand for inside each of us, their hopes and beliefs vying for dominance. We long for magic or our belief switches between fervour and doubt. In our more religious moments we try to avoid disappointment. And even when trusting strongly we pray for God to prove us right. Our efforts and faithfulness need rewarding.

The child in each of us looks for certainty. We want to be assured that the world is as we would like it to be. So we make our own worlds and play in them. But the experience is confusing. We become unsure about what we can properly desire and in what or whom we can confidently believe.

Longing and unbelief
In the Jewish and Christian traditions this mix of longing, conviction and unbelief is the mark of all religious

111

experience. The writer of Psalms 42 and 43, which are probably one psalm, beautifully expounds this theme. We long for God as a deer in the desert needs water: "As the hart longs for cooling streams so longs my soul after you, O God".

The picture puts the poet in touch with feelings which raise two contrasting questions. First, he is depressed at being separate from God. So he asks: "When shall I come into the presence of God?" Then he realizes that because he is miserable others taunt him: "Where is your God now?" And all this happens in the one place in everyday life where he could expect to find God – in the worship of the Temple liturgy.

The story of Job takes the same theme further. Job suffers, but he might be able to live with it. His comforters are not wrong. They speak to his suffering. But they are no help. Even what God says is unimportant. The reason is that the suffering is not Job's main problem. He is not perplexed by his intense suffering and because no-one can explain it. Job's quandary arises from his awful sense of estrangement from God: "O that I knew where I might find him". That need is in the end sufficiently met. God answers him with a rebuke. But that does not matter. It is the voice that counts.

Alexander Donat gives us a modern instance of the same experience. Writing of life in the wartime ghettos and camps, he does not dwell on the torment and suffering. The problem is God:

We cried for a sign [of God] . . . [But] God was not present at our indescribable predicament. We were alone, forsaken by God and men.[4]

112

Feeling abandoned and cut off from everything and everyone is worse than any agony.

God created and revealed

This experience is the paradox of faith. Dud and Pete think there should be proof. But that is not the point. The four groups around the cross, the Psalmist and Job are not much interested in proofs that God exists. But they are very concerned about whether there is anyone to respond to their cry. Are we in the end alone in worlds which we have devised? This is the great question for religious people. But it also seems to concern everyone in some way or other.

In the most hum-drum lives we are pushed towards something that goes beyond our everyday experience. We talk, for example, about love like this. "Love conquers all" is not just a motto. We believe it. It was probably written by the Latin poet Virgil. But it has become the theme of popular song as well as popular religion. In chapter 1 we saw in the story of Patrick Bateman how it develops. Love is not something simple. Whenever we love or are loved we feel that there is always something more. So amid the down to earth business of relationships, we speak of love as something greater than these. It lies beyond us or, as we might say, it transcends us.

Take another example, this time from organizations. In the daily frenzy of activity the members of a company may lose sight of what the whole set-up is for. So they call in a consultant. He may diagnose weaknesses in the organization. More importantly he provides a new reference point. The consultant deals with day-to-day concerns but at the same time stands beyond them. By using his perspective the members recover for themselves a new sense of what lies beyond – what transcends – their everyday work. What the organization is for becomes clear again. The consultant withdraws. Then people usually complain that the whole episode was a waste of time and money. "We learned what we knew already. There was nothing new." But even though they grumble, in fact they find by using this transcending reference that they can get back to their proper work. In every area of our life we seem to need points by which to orient ourselves. This is not especially a religious matter. It is a basic human need.

If we are going to embark on a search for something, we first have to recognize that we have not got it. Dud and Pete followed the obvious pattern. They looked for proof. But experience of ordinary life suggests otherwise. It is precisely because we do not have proof and feel that there can be none that we are driven towards that which transcends us. The felt absence of God presses us towards an idea of God. In order to discover God we have to face our experience of his absence.

But behind all of this a terrifying prospect: What if that were all? What if we were to discover that God really is absent? Our longing for God makes us go to great lengths to guarantee him to ourselves. There is little doubt that every image of God is partly constructed by us. So we come to this question: How can God be produced at all by the longing of his creatures? And if he is, how is he in any sense "God"?

"Almighty God" is to some extent one we create. This is one of the discoveries of this century. Many Christians still have to come to terms with it. One of the key phrases of our day is "Everybody knows". It is used about things for which people assume argument or demonstration are unnecessary. One of the things that "everybody knows" in our Western world now is that anything religious may be the hobby of a few, but is irrelevant to real life.

We "know" this because of the way in which religious belief has been "explained". Sigmund Freud pioneered psychological explanations. Karl Marx offered his famous dictum that "religion is the opium of the people". There are many others. Their ideas can be disputed in detail. But together they have quite an effect. They have shown that whatever our vision of God, we contribute to it.

To think about God we have to bring together what we feel and what God reveals. If he is only revealed to us, he will stand over against us. We shall then be in awe of him. And if God is only a product of our feelings, we may love him. But is he there? Feeling and revelation are in tension. One cannot replace the other.

The cross is a good example of a junction where feelings and revelation come together. It is certainly a place of revelation: we, like the four groups, can observe what happens. It is there for us to see. But, as we have already noticed, when we observe the cross, we cannot just watch. The cross works on our imaginations and stirs up feelings. It seems to pull us into it, so that we have to become part of its story.

But all our thinking about God is like this. He is not just out there to be admired and worshipped. Nor is God inside us, being produced by our longings and imaginations, to be handled as we wish. We need the jargon word "interaction" to describe what happens.

115

When two people meet, they interact. One does not give and the other receive. They each contribute something to one another. And both are changed. Interaction exactly describes the partnership that must exist between God and us, if we are to know him at all. The cross challenges the arrogance that claims that we create God. It also questions any sense of divine aloofness which assigns us no part in God's existence.

God inside and outside

My godson for a while would never let go of a smelly piece of blanket called "Bampty". All parents know about such cloths or teddy bears. Without it a child will not sleep or go on a journey. To lose it means disaster. A more worthy beast or another blanket will not do. These bits and pieces are amazingly powerful. The observer, even sometimes mother or father, cannot see what all the fuss is about. Yet the things obviously mean more than we can see. They stand for something beyond our reach which looms large inside the child's mind. Yet we, too, can touch them and, if we dare, wash them. They are real, not just in the mind.

> The cloth or bear comes from without from one point of view, but not so from the point of view of the baby. Neither does it come from within; it is not an hallucination.[5]

These "transitional objects", as they are known, play a key part in helping us grow from childhood to adulthood.

We are quite used to thinking of God as at the same time both beyond us and yet within. The words for this are

116

"transcendent" and "immanent". But the topic is not theoretical. This is how we experience God.

When we worship God he lies beyond us. We long to know him and strive to find him. We are aware that he transcends our world. In our prayers we confess how limited our knowledge of him is. We look to him to reveal himself through the readings, sermon, hymns, and communion. In worship we instinctively think of God as transcendent God:

> Therefore with angels and archangels, and with all the company of heaven, we laud and magnify thy glorious name, ever more praising thee, and saying: Holy, holy, holy, Lord God of Hosts, heaven and earth are full of thy glory. Glory be to thee, O Lord most high.

The opposite happens while we are going about our daily business. Then the emphasis shifts to God within. We pray for him to be immanent in us: "Make me a channel of your peace." We are less consciously aware of him, because our minds are rightly preoccupied with living. But the God of everyday and the God of worship are not separate. They are one and the same. The idea that God is inside and outside, immanent and transcendent, is a basic religious experience.

Children use transitional objects. So do adults. As babies we have the one. But when we grow up we have many. They are not so obvious, but they fill our minds. We hold onto them as our fall back positions. We revert to them, not consciously, when things get stressful.

Babies eventually abandon their objects. The indispensable teddy bear is relegated to the bottom of the toy basket.

Overnight the smelly bit of blanket is no longer needed to perform its magic. Children do not deliberately reject them. They simply cease to be important. Other things and people take their place.

But there is an exception. The idea of God seems to stay around. It seems that we get some sense of him quite early in our lives. But many, if not most, people relegate God to the rubbish cupboard of the mind. Other concerns crowd in and he is forgotten. Yet in practice he continues to drift in and out of our lives and resurfaces at critical moments.

For example, people come to church for baptism, marriage or funerals who would not dream of appearing on any other occasion. A disaster may lead nations or communities to invoke God. They may then look to the church or vicar to help them handle a moment in their lives when they feel a sense of something beyond their everyday experience.

In 1991 we saw an example from Moscow. During the night when the people confronted the tanks in front of the Parliament Building, three young men were killed. When the coup was over their funeral was held. As if from nowhere priests appeared, old hymns were sung, ancient rituals re-enacted. You could see people struggling to remember how to cross themselves.

In the face of unmanageable feelings people may rediscover some sense of God. Christians often make the mistake of thinking this experience should become permanent. They become annoyed when people come for a baptism or memorial service but do not join the church. But the felt need is usually temporary. God is being pulled out of limbo and then put back.

Many, maybe even all of us, spend our lives dealing from

time to time with some idea of God, creating and finding him. This is not necessarily the God of religious faith. We all seem to worship something or someone. Some have this experience but are not sufficiently attracted to wish to keep exploring. But for others he is endlessly fascinating and we are captivated. Most of us live somewhere in between and move up and down a scale between belief and unbelief.

R. S. Thomas describes this experience as a pilgrimage. He returns to an island where there is an ancient shrine and thinks about the first pilgrims:

> Am I too late?
> Were they too late also, those
> first pilgrims? He is such a fast
> God, always before us and
> leaving as we arrive.

And at the end of his poem he muses on the question: Is God within us or outside?

> Was the pilgrimage
> I made to come to my own
> self, to learn that in times
> like these and for one like me
> God will never be plain and
> out there, but dark rather and
> inexplicable, as though he were in here?[6]

A poet is supposed to ask such questions. But many more ordinary people also find that God cannot be easily dismissed:

Most of the time he shares the unpredictable life of the small child's teddy bear; when needed he is

119

hurriedly pulled from his resting place, hugged or mistreated, and when the storm is over, neglectfully left wherever he may happen to be.[7]

It may sound blasphemous to compare God with a teddy bear. But that is what we actually do. From time to time we drag in some idea of God from somewhere. This God exists at the same time inside us and outside us. He is not solely the product of our longings, although they contribute. He is also, as with Bampty or the teddy bear, an object.

The vulnerable God

These transitional objects and the way that they work give us a way of bringing together the God whom we know we long for and the God who stands transcendently beyond us. It is not a matter of either one or the other. Both are there whenever we think of God.

Around the cross, for instance, the crowd, the half-believers, the religious people and the disciples all contribute from their different experiences and needs to an idea of God. He might work a miracle, answer prayer and benefit believers. Put like that their visions seem dismally small. But these are the sort of things that most of us instinctively look to God for. But then each of these groups has to sort out the ideas about God which are inside them with the fact of the cross, which is outside, standing before them.

In previous chapters we have discovered how the cross impinges on our everyday experiences of life. But now we begin to face something more awesome: this cross also tests who God himself is.

To be God he must be powerful. Since he is its creator,

he transcends the world. He is beyond it and we properly address him as Almighty. But if he is to have anything to do with us without this power overwhelming us, he has also to be by divine standards, weak. Weakness is not the same as impotence. We are not discussing what we cannot know – whether God can or cannot do something. The weakness revealed in the cross is vulnerability.

God is vulnerable because he allows himself to be used. Anyone who wishes to know God can build on what little they perceive of him. Whatever we may wish God to be, he allows us to begin by treating him as that. He is "such a fast God", coming into being as we look to him, but (as we experience it) also going out of being for us. He is no less God for this. He reveals himself as this in the cross. There between the hopes of the watchers and the stark reality of Jesus' death, God is made known.

The doctrine which the church has developed from the story of the cross is the atonement. For once a technical word means what it says. "Atonement" is making "at one", bringing together things which would otherwise remain apart. We usually apply it to the way in which God reconciles himself and mankind at the cost of Christ's death. But there is another bringing together. On the cross the God we long for becomes one with the God who must always be beyond us.

Even in our most secret moments we need not look for the sort of God whom Dud and Pete decided they needed. It is not that God just does not reveal himself like that. The cross shows us why it would make no sense if he did. Such an easily known God would only feed our childish expectations. He would become a product of them rather than the transcendent one. And if that happened, interaction would become impossible between God and us. We could never even talk about him because we should practically be talking only to ourselves.

The cross tests God himself as much as it does us. How far will he go in handling the childlike, unrealistic expectations of the people he has made? On it he accepts yet another consequence of his act of creation. We, like the people around that cross on the first Good Friday, have our various expectations. In that one event they are addressed. And the God who is revealed is

> not greater than in his humiliation, not more glorious than in self-surrender, not more powerful than in helplessness, not more divine than in his humanity.[8]

He may be far from "Yoo, hoo! Here I am." But he is consequently nearer to each of us than we may often realize.

FOR DISCUSSION

1. How far are the four types around the cross found in your group today?

2. Does this way of thinking about God match your own religious experience? If so, how?

3. What would be the effects on your church if it really believed in this "vulnerable God"?

CHAPTER 5

THIBAULT'S WISDOM

A Crucified God?

Matthew 27:27–54
Another Account from Condemnation to Execution

We now read the story of the cross again, this time as Matthew told it. Neither his version nor Luke's is "right" or "wrong". The story is both history and interpretation. The Gospel writers could not think of one without the other. **A scarlet robe** (*v.* 28) would be one of the soldier's own cloaks; a **crown of thorns** (*v.* 29) would probably not have been designed, as in many pictures, to inflict pain, but was a radiant crown with the spikes going outwards; **a reed** (*v.* 29) would be a pretend sceptre; and the greeting **Hail, King!** was a parody of "Hail, Caesar!" Western tradition has made the episode one of pain and suffering. But the mocking was rather part of the process of reducing the importance of the condemned man. In his account of Jesus' death Matthew, as always, offers hints from the Old Testament. **Golgotha** (*v.* 33) is Aramaic for "skull", but the place remains uncertain. The crucifixion (*v.* 35) is only mentioned briefly. *V.* 36 is peculiar to Matthew, who may be countering suggestions that Jesus was removed from the cross before he was dead. The inscription (*v.* 37) was part of the ritual, since crucifixions were warnings to others. Most importantly for Matthew the irony of the cross is emphasized. In the following verses people, chief priests, lawyers, elders and criminals all have their say (*vv.* 38–44). They fulfil of Scripture – Psalm 22:7, 22:8 and 69:9. The account of Jesus' death closely follows that of Mark. In *v.* 46 the Hebrew of Psalm 22:1 is given. **Eli** makes possible the confusion with **Elijah** (*v.* 47). According to legend Elijah, since he had not died (2 Kings 2:9–12) was able to come to the rescue of the righteous in trouble. At the death of Jesus (*v.* 50) Matthew introduces a new set of signs, which are drawn from the Old Testament. The curtain is split like the rock at Horeb (1 Kings 19:11) and the idea of the early resurrection of the dead comes from Ezekiel 37. **After Jesus was raised from the dead** (*v.* 53) reminds readers that these omens are timeless. They are put here as foretastes of the victory of God which, as the story goes, still has to be achieved on Easter Day. That is why, for instance, it is futile to ask of *v.* 54 why such a confession was needed, since all Jerusalem by then should have believed. **Son of God** is also ambiguous. The centurion might simply have meant "a divine being". For Christian readers it is another testimony to what they believe about Jesus as the Son of God.

CHAPTER 5

Sydney Carter is a Quaker and hymn writer. He has contributed some notable new hymns to the repertoire, probably the best known being "Lord of the Dance". Another is about the crucifixion, which he views from an unusual angle. The disciples are at the foot of the cross. They look up and wonder. But Carter's singer is one of the two thieves. At Golgotha they had a unique view. All three men died side by side. The anguish and anger at what is happening is firmly laid where it belongs:

> "It's God they ought to crucify, instead
> of you and me",
> I said to the carpenter a-hanging on the
> tree.

The irony is obvious. Those singing this song already believe that on Christ's cross God is in some sense crucified. It might be that since Jesus is held to be the Son of God, we could say that God himself was crucified. Or perhaps the event is so horrific that our old images of God have been killed. In that sense God died. The ideas may become more extreme: here we see the eternal, undying one dead.

All such views have a hint of heresy about them. The guardians of orthodoxy worry. But heresy serves its purpose. It is like the husk of a seed: it eventually dies but in so doing fertilizes the kernel of a new tradition. Even if they are sometimes technically doubtful, we feel the force of such ideas. It may be heresy to suggest that God died. But the cross makes us ask what sort of God are we believing in when we contemplate it.

The final cry

The gospel accounts of the passion vary. As the earliest Christians thought about Jesus' life and death they began to interpret it in different ways. The resurrection did not change the starkness of the cross. It was as bewildering afterwards as it was before. The first version of the story to be put into order was probably in worship. At the Lord's Supper Christians proclaimed in words and actions the Lord's death (1 Corinthians 11:26). They retold the stories of Jesus' life, but now looking at them through the lenses of the cross and resurrection.

All four gospels agree that Jesus uttered a cry as he died. Luke says "Jesus cried aloud and said, 'Father, into your hands I surrender my spirit' " (Luke 23:46). A loud cry followed by a coherent prayer is not very likely from a man dying from crucifixion. The style of death was too awful for that. Breathing was the hardest task. The remains of a crucified man from Jesus' time have been discovered. Medical studies on the skeleton have shown that the probable cause of death was suffocation brought on by the lungs filling with fluid. Yet in Luke's account the dying Jesus calmly says the Good Night Prayer from Psalm 31.

John moderates the idea. For him Jesus's final words are, "It is accomplished". Then he dies (John 19:30). The writer may imply that Jesus claims that he has done all that was asked of him: "I have done everything". But more likely he wants us to think of God as the achiever: "All that God intended has been completed". If so, there may be a connection with the versions of the cry in Mark and Matthew. Both quote the beginning of Psalm 22. But that psalm ends: "They shall tell to a people yet unborn, that this was the Lord's doing" (Psalm 22:31). Maybe Mark and Matthew, like John, also wish to emphasize that God has completed his work.

But whatever the case, there is no avoiding the shock when Jesus utters the first words from Psalm 22: "My God, my God, why have you forsaken me?" The authors may mean us to think that as Jesus died he was using the whole psalm. It is a text for the time of death, including long passages about being abandoned by God. But in the end sorrow turns to joy as God's faithful servant is vindicated. If Jesus used it, he may have been confidently handing himself over to God. Or the writers may mean us to take this line on its own. It then becomes a wrenching cry of despair.

Two remarkable points emerge from this survey. First, each gospel gives Jesus the last word. Just before he dies he says something. His death does not obviously convey its meaning. The cross is such a problem that even its victim has to comment on it. Second, all the interpretations offered are ambiguous. An improbably strong voice utters a prayer that would at best be whispered (Luke); a reference to ending and success, but without any certainty as to whose (John); and the text about being abandoned by God, which might be taken literally or as a prelude to God's stepping in with power (Mark and Matthew).

This cry adds a new dimension to our thinking about the cross. So far it has opened up some of our human dilemmas and those of our world. It addresses the major questions of life. We know deep down that they have to be faced. Yet we also know that they cannot be finally answered. But Jesus's final cry, whatever the words used, explicitly brings in God. At the climax of the crucifixion there are not just the various people and Jesus. God is now named. The cross invites us to explore how it affects God himself.

The pain of God

The questions which the cross raises are never either/or but both/and. Any response that we feel to it will be ambiguous. But ambiguity pulls us apart and always involves pain. We find ourselves in two minds and feel caught between them. We are torn in two directions at once. Occasionally the soreness can feel physical. Ambiguity can literally give us a headache.

Pain and the cross are inseparable. The crucifixion counters any suggestion that suffering can be insignificant. Sometimes, however, the church has treated Christ's sufferings as only physical. This view fitted the harsh world of medieval times. So the church dwelt morbidly on the wounds. Meditations, hymns, paintings and sculptures focused on his hurt.

But the final cry seems to imply that the pain of the cross is not just physical anguish. It is more like what we would call psychological pain. There is God, who is faithful and to be trusted, the God on whom we rely. Yet that God either makes impossible demands, leading to "It is finished", or at the critical moment he proves faithless – "Why have you abandoned me?" This sort of agony goes with being in two minds. It comes from being torn apart. And if God

130

is, as we believe, somewhere in the cross, it arises for him from the way in which on the cross God denies himself and so suffers.

Luther grasped this point with typically bold comments. When he said that the test of everything is the cross, the "everything" must include God himself. We have already noted that in the story of the cross we cannot avoid the two themes of betrayal and abandonment. Now with some daring the cross invites us to ask what it might mean if we apply them to God himself.

We have already considered betrayal as "handing over". This is the principle of God's dealings with his world, as is manifest in the cross. Judas hands Jesus over to the authorities. The Jews hand Jesus over to Pilate. He hands him over to the executioners. Eventually it becomes the theme of the mission itself. The gospel is handed over to Paul and the other apostles, who in turn hand it on to us.

But abandonment is more intense than handing over. The cry of dereliction, "My God, my God, why have you forsaken me?", tells us of some kind of separation between the Father and the Son in the cross. But such language brings us near to God's nature and how it is revealed. This separation is also the point where the two of them together are most close. Since it is here that Jesus' ministry comes to its inevitable climax and where, as we believe, God achieves a major change in his world.

This language sounds strange. And the more we meditate on this theme, the more peculiar it becomes. Luther himself ended with a paradox. On the cross, he said, "No-one is against God except God himself."[1] When we let our minds roam freely around the story of the cross, we can begin

131

to feel what abandonment means and what such tearing apart might be like. We need not all worry about the theological niceties. Artists and poets will help us more.

But as we reflect, a terrible problem emerges: God begins to look as though he might be a sadist. He gives us his Son and allows him to be executed. Does that not make him Christ's murderer? If so, God seems to stand on the side of those who inflict pain. This awful thought is not made more comfortable, by his being seen at the same time as on the side of those who suffer.

A father who abuses his child does something shocking. But the fundamental horror is that he betrays a trust. He "hands over" the child for whom as father he is responsible to an irresponsible side of himself, the abuser. The story of Abraham and Isaac addresses this question. God tests Abraham by inviting him to surrender his son Isaac as a sacrifice. Until this century it was a story about the past. Most sermons still treat it as such. God was not a sadist but generous: he provides a ram, the sacrifice is complete, and Isaac lives happily ever after to populate the earth.

But this story now makes a different point. Wilfred Owen tells the familiar version up to the moment when Abraham is about to sacrifice Isaac. Suddenly an angel calls:

> Lay not thy hand upon the lad,
> Neither do anything to him, thy son.
> Behold! Caught in a thicket by its horns,
> A ram. Offer the Ram of Pride instead.
> But the old man would not so, but slew his son,
> And half the seed of Europe, one by one.[2]

This is our world. Once we have seen this we can no longer

think about God as we did before. The cross has always stood for God's generosity. He loves the world so much that he gives himself up to save it. The cross shows the lengths to which he will go. But in our age there is to such sacrifice a dark side of abuse and wrong. We cannot just accept it. We have to go further and ask how the cross tests what God's self-surrender means.

God is God, we believe, precisely because he is not affected by the sort of things that influence our lives. He does not suffer them. Nor can he take part in the abuse and wrong which permeate our sense of how the world is. But here is the paradox again: If he is not deeply involved, can God deal with our world? Yet if he is, given what we now know, what sort of God is he for any world?

Thibault's wisdom

Thibault, servant to Peter Abelard, makes clear for us what seems obscure to everyone else. Abelard was a noted teacher at the University of Paris during the twelfth century. The passion of his illicit love for his pupil Heloise is one of the great love stories of all time. It had him expelled from the university and the city. Eventually, so the story goes, he retired to the forest. There he set up a small place to live and pray, an oratory. He lived alone, except for his loyal servant, Thibault.

One evening the two of them are preparing supper. Suddenly both freeze. An unearthly scream echoes through the woods. Abelard in particular is shaken. He fears that a child is being attacked. The more experienced Thibault realizes after the second scream that it is the sound of a rabbit caught in a trap.

"A rabbit," said Thibault. He listened. "There's nothing worrying about it. It'll be in a trap. Hugh told me he was putting them down. Christ!" The scream came yet again. Abelard was beside him, and the two plunged down the bank.

"Down by the river", said Thibault. "I saw them playing, God help them, when I was coming home. You know the way they go demented with fun in the evenings. It will have been drumming with its hind paws to itself and brought down the trap."

Abelard went on, hardly listening. "O God", he was muttering. "Let it die. Let it die quickly."

But the cry came yet again. On the right, this time. He plunged through a thicket of hornbeam.

"Watch out", said Thibault, thrusting past him. "The trap might take the hand off you."

The rabbit stopped shrieking when they stooped over it, either from exhaustion, or from the last extremity of fear. Thibault held the teeth of the trap apart, and Abelard gathered up the little creature in his hands. It lay for a moment breathing quickly, then in some blind recognition of the kindness that had met it at the last, the small head thrust and nestled against his arm, and it died.

It was that last confiding thrust that broke Abelard's heart. He looked down at the little draggled body, his mouth shaking. "Thibault," he said, "do you think there is a God at all? Whatever has come to me, I earned it. But what did this one do?"

Thibault nodded.

"I know," he said. "Only – I think God is in it too."[3]

Thibault's earthy wisdom leads to more than a new way of pondering on suffering. Abelard, the theologian, immediately recognizes that it offers a new way of thinking about God. At Auschwitz we learned that when we are faced by torment it is not enough to find some sort of explanation. So with Abelard. What he first thought was child abuse turned out to be the cry of a dying rabbit.

Child abuse is a macabre torment. Most people think it worth trying to find out why it happens and to do something about it. The death of a rabbit in a trap is disturbing. But it is difficult to claim that it is as important as child abuse. This rabbit was probably destined to be Thibault and Abelard's next meal. Nevertheless, it brings us, as it brought them, face to face not just with the suffering creature. In it we encounter the Creator himself. All suffering, however relatively trivial it might seem, becomes a question about God.

Thibault and Abelard talk further. The one has the rustic honesty of someone who day to day deals in survival. The other is intellectually remote. But Abelard, the scholar, is increasingly amazed. Thibault suggests that there can be no suffering in the world which God does not feel. Even the pain of an insignificant rabbit counts. What is more, if God, as its Creator, can feel the suffering of a rabbit, he must feel it more deeply than any human being. His links with the rabbit are more intimate than ours. We look at it. We probably like it. We may even eat it and so let it do us some good. But God created it. It uniquely belongs to him. We

135

can never own it like that. And so God is in a position to love it in a way which can never be ours.

Abelard the theologian looks for a place where this could fit in his understanding of God's scheme of things. His thoughts turn first to the cross. So he asks Thibault whether he is thinking about Calvary. But Thibault is not finished. Calvary and the cross are not the whole story.

> "That is what Christ's life was; the bit of God that we saw. And we think God is like that, because Christ was like that, kind and forgiving sins and healing people. We think God is like that for ever, because it happened once, with Christ. But not the pain. Not the agony at the last. We think that stopped." . . . .
>
> "Then, Thibault," he [Abelard] said slowly, "you think that all this," he looked down at the quiet little body in his arms, "all the pain of the world, was Christ's cross?"
>
> "God's cross", said Thibault. "And it goes on."
>
> "The Patripassian[4] heresy", muttered Abelard mechanically. "But, O God, if it were true. Thibault, it must be. At least, there is something at the back of it that is true. And if we could find it – it would bring back the whole world."

The feeling side of God

In 1136 Abelard was found guilty of heresy. He appealed to Rome, but died before he could defend himself, and was buried beside Heloise. But by then he had written his theory of the atonement. We can read it in his Commentary on

Romans. But just as much about it is found in his passionate letters to Heloise. He also wrote hymns for her and her nuns to sing in the abbey. Some of these were rediscovered in the nineteenth century. We can imagine the nuns, Thibault and thousands like them humming the doctrine of the atonement:

> Our sins, not thine, thou bearest, Lord;
>   Make us thy sorrow feel,
> Till through our pity and our shame
>   Love answers love's appeal.[5]

When with Thibault and Abelard we stand before the cross, three points arise. First, we learn that we must never use religious beliefs or theological difficulties to protect ourselves from reality. The world's torment is genuine. If we believe in God, this anguish cannot be separated from some idea of God's pain. Abelard was right, as he listened to Thibault, to whisper "Patripassianism". As a scholar he thought in theological terms. He could not think without them and needed the correct word. But he could not let his learning contradict what he felt.

Perhaps that is why he could only whisper the word. He was caught: he knew he was right and he knew he was wrong. The pain of the world, felt by the rabbit, joined his own inner pain from losing Heloise. Then it dawned on Abelard: love can only be poured out. So when God reveals himself as love – that is, when he hands himself over to us, his creatures – he must suffer. Whatever the theories say, while there is any pain in the world, there is also pain in God.

Second, he emphasized that whenever we think about

the cross we cannot deny our experience. Love is a basic human experience. Abelard's ardour for Heloise comes out in all his writing. He knew how intense passion is. And he also knew what it costs. But this experience was so deep in him that he could not think of the cross apart from it.

In one passage he invites Heloise to think of herself as a bystander as Jesus passes on his way to his death. Many a spiritual director has done the same. But Abelard goes further. Heloise is not an observer. Because of where she stands she has to be a participant. Really to see the cross is like being in love. You cannot be dispassionate. Like a magnet it both pulls us towards it and repels us.

Thirdly, Abelard once and for all demonstrates that no mechanical scheme of how the cross makes us at one with God and our neighbour can ever work. Some theories have involved calculating benefit and cost. Payments and receipt have been balanced. But all of them become arid because they are inhuman. The cross has to be a place of feeling and imagination. When we allow it to work on this level, it transforms lives. In Abelard's thinking love, the emotion which rejects balance and equation, becomes the touchstone.

Religious people usually invoke the word "mystery" too easily. But in connection with the cross it points us in the right direction. Mysteries are felt. They are never understood. The point is made in the stories of the crucifixion. Notice the feelings of the people involved. As Jesus moves nearer the cross the people around him become more rounded characters. Up to this point the gospels tell us about people like healed lepers, a young ruler or a Syrophoenician woman. Nearly all are anonymous. What were they like? How did Jesus affect them? We speculate but are not given any of the details we should like to know.

But when the passion drama begins we learn a lot about the characters. They have names and show feelings: nervous Pilate and his anxious wife; the priests and their jealousies; Joseph of Arimathea, the man of secret faith. Peter and Judas reveal their characters. Even a servant is given a special role and eventually a name, Malchus.

The people around the cross become like us. Like Heloise we watch. But we are not just observers. Those caught up in the drama act out our lives before us. But there is even more. As Abelard began to realize, when our feelings as creatures are aroused like this, we have to go further. We have to dare ask about the Creator's feelings and find ourselves riskily nudging the feeling side of God. If the cross really tests everything, that "everything" includes this mystery: What does the cross mean for God himself?

Even to raise the question sounds presumptuous. Spiritual tradition requires human beings to know their place:

> How you confuse things, as if the potter were no more important than the clay! Shall what is made say about its maker, "He did not make me"? Can the pot say of the potter, "He has no skill"? (Isaiah 29:16).

Dare a human being answer God back? The cross answers "yes". Such behaviour is not audacious when we stand before the cross. Everything about it is public. So when we ask what it means for God, we can expect a reply.

A window into God

The image of Jesus as a window into God is a risky one. It might imply that we can observe God without becoming involved ourselves. But if we ever thought that, we now know differently. We have re-discovered that we learn best by taking part. Children at school immerse themselves in projects. Adult educationalists make people do things. We change as we learn as we participate.

Imagine the cross as a window into God. A window works in two directions. We look out through it; and it also lets light into the room. We have already thought about how the cross sheds light on our experiences of freedom, responsibility and guilt. But now we look the other way, out from our lives into God, the source of that light.

Every effective action involves cost. We daily expend energy, time and money to get things done. When Jesus' final cry interprets what is happening to him, it emphasizes achievement. The cross is God's work. And the window of the cross allows us to glimpse how God works and at what cost to himself. And the cost turns out to be his being pulled apart. Far from being heretical, Thibault's insight is confirmed.

Splitting as self-protection

Dealing with the unfamiliar always disturbs us. We instinctively react by trying to keep ourselves free of anything strange. We do this with people. We label those who make us uncomfortable as "them". They contrast with the "us" we think we know. We divide black from white, or workers from bosses, or men from women. This sort of splitting is around when any group is described as "they".

The mass media, for example, present all life as a dramatic struggle. Politics are the conflict between two parties, often of two people. Difficult moral issues arise, which have to be resolved in a few seconds. So opposite positions, which probably no-one actually holds, are presented to force a conclusion. We like to think that we are quite sophisticated. But we cannot help seeing things in twos, them and us. In our world the goodies always fight the baddies. And we are invariably sure which side we are on.

Splitting sounds mean and wrong. Even if people behave like this, surely Christians should not condone it. There should be no "them" and "us". But this sort of splitting is in fact our normal human way of behaving. It is not a weakness or a sin. It is simply the way we manage overwhelming stress or the sort of anxiety which seems destructive.

Marriage, for example, is an intimate relationship between two people. They are attracted to each other for all sorts of reasons. Then trouble arises, so the couple seeks help. They go to a counsellor and talk about each other and their marriage. More often than not their pictures are simplified. One partner is accused of being frigid. So the other is lusty. Or it may be money: one is stingy, so the other is generous. Life with other people may cause them problems: one is sociable, so the other is a recluse.

When things are normal both partners take their share in all this. Each is more or less frigid and lusty, stingy and generous, sociable and reclusive. As we say, it depends how we feel. Marriage is a mixture of such stances. But when it comes under stress, the relationship begins to break up. Each partner loses touch with themselves. The husband, for instance, sees the faults in his wife but not in himself. He cuts himself off from them. She will be doing the same. The partners defend themselves from each other in order to avoid being responsible for what they are and what is happening. This is splitting. Counsellors may point it out. It can be interpreted. But it will not go away. It makes us human.

The split in ourselves is between what is "I" and "Not-I". Through the window of the cross we can see something similar in God. There is "God" and "Not-God". We often have a sense that a rift runs through everything. In the world at large, as well as ourselves, the positive is separated from what is negative. This attitude also affects our beliefs. The more firmly we believe in God the more we find ourselves facing the problem of Not-God.

For example, God, we say, is good. He is the source of love, joy and peace. This is the language of faith and worship, those moments when we are conscious of God. But what about the negatives – the "Not-God" of hatred, misery and disharmony? These are as much components of this world, which God has made, as the good.

Some religion, as we have already seen, copes by separating the two. For instance, God either struggles with evil or constructs a harmony of opposites. But as Abelard realized, we cannot think about God without acknowledging how important our feelings are. Since we know that splitting is basic to our make-up, we now must bring together our sense of "I" and "Not-I" with our thinking about God as both "God" and "Not-God". If we loosen either of these tensions, we diminish God or deny what we are.

God's splitting as self-surrender

The cross is God's assurance that we are moving in the right direction when we think like this. Crucifixion speaks of being torn apart or split. The victim's body was rent. If the cross did not succeed, the soldiers were sent with spears to make sure. The cross is also public. Since no crucifixion could be private, God's cross stands as his public invitation to examine what he is doing. And there is no doubt that the cross is an evil. So the themes of splitting, public scrutiny, good and evil are all brought together in the cross.

At this point, tutored by Thibault, we are not talking in general terms about the facts of the cross. We are asking what it reveals about God. The window of the cross now invites us to look out of it into who God is and what he does. What we see is that splitting which we already know in our own experience. As he dies, Jesus cries out: "My God, my God, why have you abandoned me?" Christians believe that God has revealed himself in Jesus. The final point of revelation is that Jesus becomes the split off part of God. And we can even grasp something of what that means for God, even though it remains a mystery. Because the sight shows that one of our most fundamental human experiences is also found in the heart of God himself.

But there is a major difference between God and us. We always use splitting to defend ourselves. We shut off aspects of ourselves, usually those we do not like, so that we do not have to face them. We load them onto other people, complain about them, and so save ourselves from being disturbed. We defend ourselves but at cost to other people. If God does the same, there is no hope. He would only be like us. But as Thibault felt, and Abelard worked out, there is a difference. The splitting which is for us a normal defence becomes for God the point where he shows that he is never defensive.

We often put into God parts of ourselves that we cannot

cope with. He gets blamed for our problems, uncertainties and anxieties. When people do this to us, we resist. But God is different. Caught up in the same sort of behaviour, he does not fight back. Instead, as the cross demonstrates, he allows himself to be used and publicly endures the destructiveness and pain that follow. He turns the process on its head. God does not protect himself by locating all that is wrong and evil in someone else. Instead he accepts both God, all that is creative, and Not-God, all that is destructive, in himself.

That is what we mean when we say that God saves us. He holds the splits in himself, so that we are not cut off from him. He is torn apart in order to give us a vision of wholeness. We are invited to look through the window of the cross. There in God we see things which are all too familiar – ambiguity, pain, splitting and absurdity. But like Thibault and Abelard in the forest we also glimpse a new world which is not beyond us.

God's atonement

The cross can give guilty, split, tormented souls a glimpse of what wholeness means for God. This is not held up as an ideal which we cannot attain. God becomes defenceless at the very point where in our lives we find such behaviour most difficult. Because he is so close to us, we are given hope that change is possible. Our natural defensive splitting can be made positive.

In Bunyan's *Pilgrim's Progress*, Christian, the pilgrim, is on the grand journey from this world to the next. Stumbling along a narrow way, hemmed in on both sides, he comes to a hill. On it stands the cross, below which is a tomb.

Just as *Christian* came up with the *Cross*, his burden was loosed from his Shoulders, and fell from off his back; and began to tumble; and so continued to do, till it came to the mouth of the Sepulcher, where it fell in, and I saw it no more.

Then was *Christian* glad and lightsom, and said with a merry heart, *He hath given me rest, by his sorrow; and life, by his death.*[6]

Glimmers of how this new life comes about appear in the gospel stories of the passion. The disciples, for instance, are divided among themselves. In disarray and separated from their leader, they appear aimless. As a group they are all ready to blame one another. They are ripe for the normal style of human behaviour – defensive splitting and its destructive effect. Then they again tell each other the story of the crucifixion. They begin to glimpse how on the cross God was himself torn apart. As they focus on this wonder, God begins to work on them. The story-tellers feel less disturbed and are drawn together. They regroup around the retold cross and spot God in the appalling things that have happened. Reconciled to one another they start to proclaim the Gospel in their style of living as much as what they say.

One story from the Passion carries this theme beyond the disciples and any individual. When Jesus dies the veil of the temple is torn apart. This story probably refers to the curtain which hung between the Holy of Holies, where God dwelt, and the rest of the temple. As it is rent, a new access to God is opened up. It is like a window opening.

But this can only happen at a cost to God himself. The Holy of Holies represents God's presence in the world.

When the curtain is torn, the relationship between God and his world is altered. He is no longer quite so hidden. One of his old securities, his mystery, has been taken away. At the point where God and his people meet he now becomes vulnerable.

A relationship here is changing. But as we have seen, when relationships change, splitting is most likely to occur. But in this story no one is blamed. God, represented by the Holy of Holies, and Not-God, represented by all that was kept out by the curtain, do not fly apart. The reverse happens: they are brought together. God holds this split in himself and a great divide is healed. The Temple and the curtain had been erected by the Jewish people. It was an important aspect of their understanding of what God was like. But when the curtain is torn away, that way of thinking about God is changed for ever. We have to rethink everything. The church has been doing so since that day.

But there is another very practical effect. As the curtain is removed, the Holy of Holies and the rest of the Temple are brought together. So we who are God's because he made us, who occupy the outer courts of the Temple, and those who are God's because he chose them, whose representative alone may enter the Holy of Holies, become one. Because God does not defend himself, various people are saved, divided classes are brought together, and the new world comes into being. Destructive splitting is transformed and becomes creative.

The test of God

We have had a glimpse of how the cross tests God himself. He has always been naturally self giving. A creator could be nothing less. Now this generosity is pressed to the limit. In the cross we see God split between what is God and what is Not-God. One option would have been to leave the division outside himself and preserve himself as pure. All that is false in his world could be labelled "Not-God" and ignored. But his work on the cross is radically different. His style of behaviour is one which we understand only too well. But unlike us he accepts the pain of holding the split in himself and allows others to use him.

> But, O God, if it were true. Thibault, it must be. At least, there is something at the back of it that is true. And if we could find it – it would bring back the whole world.

We began this chapter with Sydney Carter's song. The paradox is now clearer. The dying thief was not just talking with the carpenter of Nazareth. When he made his complaint against God, God was already remedying it.

About one hundred years after Jesus' death, a pagan called Justin became a Christian. He later died for his faith. Justin Martyr wrote two Apologies, or arguments for the truth of Christianity. The cross was a severe obstacle as the church began to make its way in the world. People, however intrigued by the Gospel, could not believe in a God who was involved in crucifixion. To claim that a crucified man stood in second place to the unchangeable and eternal God, Creator of the world was madness.

The cross invites us to ask whether, as we look through that window, we can believe our own eyes. Is there a limit to God's willingness to be used? The answer from the cross is that there is not. And one who is so used, can never be an abuser. And as Justin clearly saw and powerfully argued, no-one is in "second place". On the cross we behold a crucified God.

FOR DISCUSSION

1. We have reached the heart of the matter: why did Christ die? What answers can you now offer?

2. How does the idea of a crucified God affect your thinking about Christian worship and living?

3. Does the theme of abuse in the cross have anything to offer our world and the abuses which we find in it?

CHAPTER 6

ORESTES' RESCUE

What does it Mean to be Saved?

John 19:17–30
The Third Version from Condemnation to Death

Finally we read yet another version of the crucifixion. John's account is stripped down: many details are omitted. The calm is eerie as a majestic Jesus moves towards and onto the cross. **Carrying his own cross** (*v.* 17) is not as impossible as it sounds. The stakes of a cross were left at the place of crucifixion; the condemned man carried the cross-piece. Pilate's unusual decisiveness over the inscription **This is the King of the Jews**(*v.* 22) is to make it clear to all concerned (the three languages) that this is the ground on which the Gospel continues to be proclaimed even after the crucifixion. All nations have to hear it and respond. John elaborates the story of the parting of the garments (*vv.* 23ff.) and leaves room for our imagination. What is the significance of **four pieces**? Why a **seamless robe**? But we should not overlook the key point that this is God's plan as foretold in Scripture being fulfilled by the unwitting soldiers (*v.* 25), not by the disciples. **The disciple whom he loved** (*v.* 26) appears five times in the gospel, but we do not know who he was. He represents closeness and faithfulness to Jesus. **I thirst** (*v.* 28) matches the other gospels, except that here, as always in John, Jesus is in charge and takes the initiative. **Hyssop** (*v.* 29) is a notable problem. As a plant it would not have been stiff enough to hold a sponge. But as a symbol it takes us back to the Passover, where it was used for sprinkling the blood on the door posts. **It is finished** (*v.* 30 – and see *v.* 28) is John's greatest contribution to thinking about the cross. But

even here Jesus remains in command – he **lowered his head
and surrendered his life**.

CHAPTER 6

One of Bristol Cathedral's greatest treasures is its Saxon stone. The carving shows Christ holding a cross. To it clings a small figure, possibly a pregnant woman. His foot tramples down a demon. The slab vividly portrays the story of the Harrowing of Hell. According to this Christ, after his crucifixion but before his resurrection, visited and conquered the realm of the devil and his demons. But here are no spirits, fires, devils and toasting forks. This is a positive story. By his cross Christ lifts Eve, the mother of all and pregnant with us, from the grasp of the Destroyer. Rescue, says the artist, is central to the Christian Gospel. The religious word for this is "salvation".

The closer we get to the cross the larger it looms. We have seen how it measures us, our world, and eventually God himself. The climax of God's self-giving is seen in the lowest form of disgrace, a crucifixion. These sorts of thing are often said. But unless the cross achieves change, which is what we mean by "salvation", then these are all so many pious words.

Scapegoat and sacrifice

Actual crucifixions are rare today, although the idea is not. The football manager, for example, whose team is heavily beaten, instinctively says "We were crucified". The same is true of the scapegoat. Workers with distressed families talk of "scapegoating". The members load all their problems onto one, so as to save themselves. It is not by chance that this ancient concept is used. The image of the scapegoat sent into the wilderness speaks to something deep which is still part of our experience.

The mother of a handicapped child may lovingly say, "He's worth every sacrifice". We know what she means. Che Guevara was a famous Latin American revolutionary. "Redeem" was one of his favourite words. He spoke of "the struggle of the people to redeem itself" and "we constitute at this moment the hope of unredeemed America". Once speaking of a dead colleague he said, "His blood was shed in Bolivia, for the redemption of the exploited and the oppressed."[1] His audience then, and we now, understand the sacrifice that he was talking about.

The themes of sacrifice and scapegoat explain why substitution still underlies much thinking about the cross. Some traditional ideas about it no longer work. We have already seen that any substitute that replaces me and which I do not choose demeans me. So it cannot save. But the thought of someone being a scapegoat which carries aspects of me is not unfamiliar. Nor is the idea that in order for me to live, sometimes others make sacrifices.

The scapegoat first appears in the darkest recesses of Old Testament religion. Two pure goats were chosen. One was sacrificed to the God, Jehovah. The priest laid hands on the other – the scapegoat – and transferred to it the sins of the people. This goat was sent out into the desert to be dealt with by the mysterious demonic figure of Azazel.

It is strange that so primitive a notion has come alive again in our age. But the whole idea touches something deep inside us. It deals with what happens when our ordinary behaviour becomes malign. It is not for nothing that psychiatrists, therapists and social workers speak about scapegoating. They are used to dealing with disturbed people. But sometimes the disturbance defies psychological explanation. It seems to be deliberately perverse. To handle this they need this primitive religious language.

But there is a serious weakness when we use the term today. Our society no longer enacts the ritual of the scapegoat. So we lack a framework of symbols when we use the idea. The people of Israel had the one annual scapegoat and knew where they were when they handled it. We neither have the ritual nor are we sure about scapegoating. Unlike the Israelites, we rush all the time to load blame onto other people. And because we do not have the ritual structure of the yearly victim, we keep manufacturing new scapegoats. The history of persecution alone proves that.

If a scapegoat is to carry away offences, we have first to acknowledge them. Our dilemma is that we scarcely know how to do this, since we are unclear about whom or what we have offended. The scapegoat did not just remove the sins of individuals who may have committed them wittingly or unwittingly. It also carried away the sinfulness of the people as a whole. Each year as the felt volume of sinfulness relentlessly built up, the ritual came around to deal with it. In our world we have a similar sense of the inevitable build up of wrong. The idea of the scapegoat, maybe even the longing for one, persists. But we have no obvious ritual as a means of bringing the two together.

Breaking fate

The fact of evil is disturbing enough. But the way it persists is even more scary. About five hundred years before Jesus a Greek playwright wrote three plays about this problem. In them Aeschylus introduces us to Orestes. His story is one of inescapable fate and whether anything can be done about it. It is a question which any gospel must also address.

Orestes was born into a murderous family. The rules required each new generation to take revenge on the last. This chain of fate was unbroken and unbreakable. Eventually Orestes' turn comes. He is doomed to commit murder and does so. The first two plays explain how the sequence of vengeance developed and why justice demanded that it should continue.

In the final play Orestes is cowering in the Temple of Apollo. Around him the Furies swirl and howl. These are macabre figures. Their job is to drive men on their predetermined, but right, course of action. They are a bit like our conscience. Orestes is hopelessly stuck. He cannot deny that he has committed murder. To claim that he was fated is no defence; he knows that he did it. And he cannot escape the prodding of the Furies.

Like all good stories, this one can be read on many levels. But it rings bells with some of the worst aspects of our lives. Orestes is like each of us. We can feel trapped in a relentless cycle of offence, judgement, and further offence. Our consciences prick and sometimes frighten us. His story focuses on our behaviour: Why are we wicked? Is it because of some basic fault in each of us? Is heredity or environment to blame? Are we fated to do wrong?

Since Aeschylus's time we have learned more about ourselves. Modern studies tell us that many offenders are likely to have been offended against. Hurt themselves they hurt someone else. The cycle continues. And Orestes' story is not over yet.

Can such a chain be broken? The Greeks felt the agony of this question. They called those terrible Furies who drove men on "The Blessed Ones". They spoke nicely about them because they knew it was better not to offend them. At the first performance of the play, when these Furies appeared women miscarried and old men died. They were terrified when they gazed upon the abyss of the human heart.

Can Orestes be acquitted? We go back to the story. The jurors of the city are summoned to try the case. In court the arguments rage. Old and new orders clash. The final vote is even: six for acquittal and six against. The system seizes up and cannot cope with the situation. Then Athene, the patron goddess of the city, plays her part. She casts her vote to acquit Orestes. She does not do so lightly. Everyone knows that her divine act overturns the existing order.

Life will now become more complicated as a result. By Athene's act judgement has ceased to be automatic. Even if the old way was terrible, at least we knew where we stood. Now we are less sure. The system used to guarantee a sure context for living. Now we have to examine ourselves and reach our own decisions. After Athene's vote the tension between judgement and mercy and all the other marks of our complex world have arrived for ever.

The basic fault

The story of Orestes is about disarray. When we lose a sense of order in ourselves or the world, the age old issues of evil and sin emerge again. We have already seen at Auschwitz that we cannot cope without some idea of evil, even if this is not a normal part of our way of thinking any more. The same is now true of sin.

"Sin" and "evil" are no longer everyday words. We do not instinctively use them. We look for gentler language. "Integration" has become a popular theme. If, the argument runs, we can put two parts of the world together, things will be better. If we attune ourselves to nature, a harmonious world order will be established. The same is claimed for individuals. We need to discover how female and male complement one another. And should we ever get the left and right sides of the brain together and unite its imaginative side with its logical part, we shall become new people in a new world.

Such approaches are attractive. But they all fail because they claim to make simple things that inside ourselves we know are always complex. We struggle through life with a confused mix of thoughts, feelings and actions. Simplify this mixture and you destroy life. Yet we persist in trying to reduce the combination of sin, evil, guilt, confession and forgiveness to a single scheme. With counsellors we look for causes, examine them and seek a resolution. Churches sometimes do the same under the guise of confession and absolution. Even there confession has declined to platitudes: "We are truly sorry." Mild feelings of having been wrong do not help when we have a genuine sense of offence. There is something more which has to be dealt with.

The same is true of society as a whole. A young man was charged with rape and released on bail. While in local authority care he raped two more women. The official report on the incidents said: "Society has appeared to have failed to have helped him . . ." Phrases like "the sick society" are not very clear. Like the report, they simplify things that deep down we feel are genuinely complicated.

Whether, therefore, we start with ourselves or our society, another sort of explanation is required. Our solutions are far from that network of cause and effect, offence and responsibility, guilt and impotence which enmeshed Orestes. Yet we still feel that his world is in many ways ours. And like him we need a way of interpreting what is happening to us and what we are doing.

The system demanded that Orestes should conform to its demands. His task was to carry on the fated line of vengeful killing. But behind this man who was servant of the system stood Orestes the person. The task was that of routine vengeance, his role within it was to kill, and his personal inclinations were to refuse. They coincided in a complicated network. The answer to any one of these three aspects could never solve the whole problem.

Like Orestes we might see that we are responsible for what we do. But like him, too, we feel other influences which are beyond our control: "It is just me, but it is also not just me." The General Confession in the Book of Common Prayer catches the point in its old language: "We have left undone those things which we ought to have done; And we have done those things which we ought not to have done." Personal responsibility – "We have" – comes first. But the word "ought" reminds us that we feel demands are made on us which we have to manage.

In the course of our life we engage in many tasks. We have to do thousands of different things. Some we choose; many are foisted on us. Because of them we are also expected to be something. For example, we find ourselves in a family.

This has its tasks, such as, for instance, enabling children to grow up. In that family we will have our role, perhaps as father or mother. Wives or husbands, workers or unemployed, Christians or not Christians, we occupy a myriad of such roles during our lifetime. Add to these our individual personality, and we begin to see why in every role there is scope for error. We know that we never quite get it right.

The tasks we are set, the roles expected of us, and who we ourselves are together make up the context for sin. Traditionally sin has been thought of as an offence against God. But today many people have little or no sense of God. They cannot conceive what it might be to offend against him or his laws. But they still have some awareness of sin, even though the word is not used. It comes to us through the way we behave in our many roles in life. We are trapped between knowing what is required of us and being unable to act in that way. Not everyone sees that they may have offended against God. But we all know what it is to ruin a task which we know we ought to carry out.

"Sin" describes what happens when we behave without integrity in any of our roles. People quite reasonably expect us as father, mother, teacher, Christian and so on, to live responsibly with them. Yet we all know that we can never live up to those expectations. Why we so easily lose such integrity remains obscure. The basic fault just is. But we also know when we have offended people. We feel it in ourselves and know that we have to deal with the consequences.

The old story of the Fall makes the point. Something has to start things off, so the serpent tempts Eve. But after that the snake is no longer important. Sin now lies in what Adam and Eve do. Once they have knowledge of good and evil, they are also aware of themselves within God's world. What they have hitherto done instinctively, now becomes a matter of decision. There is, therefore, plenty of room to get things wrong. Roles as male and female, worker and child-bearer, agents of God and so on are assigned to them. The original cause, whatever it was, is left behind. How they behave in these roles becomes the central issue.

For us, too, any original causes for our behaviour are left behind as we progress through life. It may sometimes be helpful to uncover some of the reasons why we behave as we do. But alone these are not enough. The search directs us into the private world of ourselves, from which it is difficult to escape. We have already seen with Sammy Mountjoy that we sense in the here and now of our lives what sin is and for what we need forgiving. We have to seek it from those we have wronged. This much is familiar and undoubtedly hard. But if this were all, our lives could, perhaps with a bit of help, be quite manageable.

But we also know that the impact of what we do goes far beyond anything or anyone that we know. We can and do offend against people we never meet. Only later may the true extent of what we have done appear. Certainly we can never ask their forgiveness. Then there is no escape from our sin against them. What exactly is it? Who can forgive us for it? The original cause, if ever discovered, has long gone. There is no-one left to forgive us for that. But we still know that we need forgiving.

Orestes crouching in the temple knew this. If he turned to the past and the first cause, he would simply end up locked into the world of fate. If he refused to do what was required of him, he would let himself down in his own eyes, as well as in the eyes of others. He knew and felt in his misery that there is more to our offences than we realize or usually admit.

The range of offence is vast. Indeed, we could say that it is without limit. We do not need a notion of law to make us feel that we have offended. We are so aware of people and our effect on their lives, that, as our vision grows larger, so our sense of offence becomes greater. So unlimited and undefined a sense of sin calls for one to forgive who is also without limit. The scapegoat was such in the ancient world. The only scapegoat in our age who is large enough is God himself. If the enormity of felt sin is to be dealt with, a matching largeness of God alone can do it.

Sin and evil

But there is another level to our behaviour which takes us beyond sin or offence. This is corruption. A corrupt person deliberately sets out to serve their own ends at the expense of others. He or she may hope that people might not notice. But they themselves know what they are trying to do.

Most of us live at the level of sin. We make excuses for why we do or do not do things. Some of these are more believable than others. But we know that we are responsible, whatever allowances we and others may make, for our behaviour and its unseen consequences. Corrupt behaviour is more than offence. The corrupt person, by contrast with the sinner, has a deliberate aim and works towards known consequences for his actions. When we think of corruption we come face to face with our motivations. These distinctions are not exact. But we are now in the borderland between offence, which is sin, and corruption which is evil.

For example, consider Adolf Hitler. He was probably not more or less of a sinner than many other people. But he was evil. It gradually became clear to the world that he deliberately intended to treat people as expendable. He used Jews, Russians, dissidents, homosexuals, disabled people and others to create his own ideal world. Eventually people throughout Europe and the rest of the world grasped what was happening. But they were not facing a sinner, so they knew that they could not just forgive him. Hitler represented something more than offence. It was evil.

You cannot forgive evil; it has to be borne. As it became more obvious what Hitler was doing, the nations discovered that they could not do much. Their only option was to resist. So they went to war. Inside Germany the same decision was made by those who plotted against Hitler. They, too, could not forgive. This was not a suitable way of responding. They also had to defy evil. People inside and outside Germany had to endure evil and deal with it as best they could. In the end it was purged. But this was not a process of forgiveness. Only when evil had been defeated could the particular sins and offences of individuals be forgiven.

But such a thought seems appalling. If evil can only be borne, then torment must be endured. But, as we saw when thinking about Auschwitz, to endure does not mean merely to accept. Evil can be resisted. But it cannot be forgiven. Forgiveness is the wrong level of response. When motivations are corrupted, whatever we do contributes to a relentless cycle of piling evil upon evil.

But even this cycle can be transformed and become more of a spiral. Individuals, nations and societies go round again and again, repeating familiar experiences. The same is true of the cross. Christ was once crucified. But he is also re-crucified. What happened to him occurs again and again. But faith based on this cross sees that each time we go round the cycle things move slightly. We do not come back to quite the same place. We have moved on to another level on a spiral. We gain a new perspective. Even evil can be transformed into the basis for positive change. Reflecting on the evil of Hitler, we might wonder whether the new hope of Europe could have emerged without that evil having been endured and resisted.

In the face of sin, the cross stands for forgiveness. We have already explored this with Sammy Mountjoy. Hamlet's play showed how the proclaimed cross could bring about change. We have also seen that God is there both revealed and tested. The cross stands, as we seek forgiveness, for God's infinite capacity to forgive. It offers us a pattern, so that we can forgive others. And it is the source of forgiveness for all those sins which seem unforgivable, because we can never know the extent of our offence.

Evil, too, is addressed. The cross is without doubt itself evil. As God forgives us our sins he also offers us a way of living which acknowledges both that evil is real and that something can be done about it. The cross shows that to bear evil is not a surrender to it. The action of the cross is seen in the people that it changes, many of whom we have met in the course of this book. It is also seen in the changed world in which we now, albeit often ignorantly, live.

The ritual of the cross

This chapter is about salvation, what God does. Being saved

is not gaining a new status and feeling happy. It is, as Orestes recognized, about being released from a life that seems fated and so being able to live differently. We have to live practically with sin and evil on a day to day basis. We can, therefore never describe the saved life in detail. It will always take its own shape according to who we are and the setting in which we are living. But at the end of our thinking about the cross we can discern one distinctive mark of Christians. For the crucified Christ and for his followers others are always their first point of reference. We live and die on behalf of others.

Ritual is meant to enable us to do that. People still use the idea of the scapegoat. But without a sense of the ritual that lies behind the word, the scapegoat's practical value would decay. Confession is another example. The ritual is an important part of the process. We are invited to confess, even when we are not in the mood or cannot think of any particular reason to do so. Even today's new religion of personal attention, the counselling session, needs its ritual.

I watched Sophocles' *Oedipus Rex* with a psychoanalyst friend. Oedipus is central to Freud's theories. My friend was a highly qualified Freudian. He thought that he knew the story well. Yet he was moved to tears by the richness of the play and its insights into human behaviour. He had never seen them before. The Freudian reading had taken one facet of the story. It had dissected and elaborated it. In the end it had lost contact with the original. The ritual of the drama re-enacted was needed to bring new life to one of his essential concepts.

The power of the cross, too, can decline if Christians overlook its ritual effect. From the first the cross has been an acted rite. Every crucifixion was a ceremony. Since it was intended to deter people from crime, the centurion in charge had to ensure that it was done by the book. Everything was done to order. The gospel accounts make it clear that Jesus' crucifixion was not an exception.

Today the ritual of the cross is still maintained through worship. In the Eucharist, for example, we meditate on the cross, we tell the story and re-enact it. By doing so we picture it and allow it to affect us. It becomes the model by which we live. Each time we recall the cross we discover a new way of orientating ourselves in our confusing world. For a moment things appear different.

In Edwin Muir's poem *Transfiguration* the disciples on the mountain are shaken by the vision. They sense, but cannot understand, a change both in themselves and in the whole universe. But:

> Reality or vision, this we have seen.
> If it had lasted but another moment
> It might have held for ever! But the world
> Rolled back into its place, and we are here,
> And all that radiant kingdom lies forlorn,
> As if it had never stirred.

This is worship. We receive a glimpse of something different. Then everything falls back into place and life goes on. This is how the ritual of the cross keeps working. As we have seen, it can never be cut off from the realities of this world. If we try to do that, it comes back to us with its down to earth story. But when we let it free in our imaginations it gives us new visions and different ways of seeing ourselves and our world.

The cross as common ground

Worship which is focused in the cross can never be a private matter between us and God. The cross was and remains public. One intriguing question about the beginning of the church is this: How did the crucified Jesus come to be placed alongside God in worship? What actually happened is not clear. But we know that Christians soon began to pray to God "through Jesus Christ our Lord". By doing this they blurred the boundaries between God and Jesus. The cross gives us a clue, because the worshipped Jesus was always the crucified.

A crucified man became a non–person. Usually the corpse was left unburied; Jesus was an exception. This was a further disgrace, one of the ways that the victim became less than human. Crucifixions took place at a conspicuous place: a crossroads where people passed, a theatre or, as in the case of Jesus and the two bandits, on a hill. The crucified man's nothingness was there for all to see. People might mock but they were warned.

In AD 70 after a long war the Roman Emperor Titus captured Jerusalem. The soldiers stormed through the Temple to the Holy of Holies, looking for the god who had inspired the Jews to such resistance. They were astounded to find it empty. How could no-God have inspired such resistance for so long?

The surprise continues in Christian worship. God invites us to enter his presence, his Holy of Holies. But when we arrive, all we find is the crucified Jesus. And he is a non-person; that is, nothing. Whenever we pray or do anything "through Jesus Christ our Lord" we affirm what Titus found: a space.

The Romans never understood this. But we can now see that the empty space is the non-person who was crucified. We naturally get worried about who we are, what roles we possess, what people think of us, and all the other anxieties that life arouses in us. But unlike us Jesus Christ does not take up personal space. What this means becomes clearer: where there is nothing there is space for everyone. Owned by no-one, it can be open for anyone. Christian worship, the most intimate act of believers, is always public and is like common ground. Everyone can stake their claim to it.

The non-person hangs on the cross to make sure that we never forget that. The rituals of worship cannot belong to us. They are there for others. Through them we keep alive on behalf of others ideas, thoughts, images and ways of living, like sacrifice and the scapegoat, which otherwise would decay.

St Paul explains dramatically what this means in Galatians 2:20. He bases his Christian living on the phrase "Not-I but Christ". We human beings are always making claims. We fill up space in people's lives and control access to our own. But those who in worship follow the way of the cross have that "I" replaced by the Christ. He, the crucified, is our example of what "Not-I" means. This is not a negative sort of self-denial but a positive way of living for others. Because Jesus on the cross became "Not-I", there is room at that cross for each one of us with our distinctive personality and psychological make up. And no one can exclude any on the grounds that they do not fit. Nor can they control access to God. At his heart lies for ever this public, common ground.

Many people feel that they have a claim on the churches'

time and ministry. People come for a variety of reasons and
not all formally belong. No minister ever knows why they
come. Indeed, most worshippers themselves do not know
exactly why. When asked they usually reply, "It's proper"
or "It's right". This is how people may practically use the
common ground. Because they are open spaces of the
Gospel, everyone has a right to be there. The churches'
ministry is to tend the space.

Once Christians grasp this vision, we are free to explore
the surrounds. We have already thought about the way in
which the Holy of Holies did not stand in isolation in the
Temple. Different courts surrounded it. Daily life went on
in some, like the Court of the Gentiles or the Court of All
Nations. Different groups were allowed into them. But at
the centre was the Holy of Holies.

Without this, the other courts would have been untended.
But because the Holy of Holies was there, the Temple was
never neutral. All its different parts pointed to God. And
because of the Holy of Holies the priests were always there
to enable people to be met by God. Christian worship is
like the Holy of Holies. Its ritual ensures that God can never
be wholly ignored. Christians worship on behalf of others
who may not. It is "a sacrifice of praise". We follow the
Christ who similarly died for others, whether they followed
him or not.

When at the end of his journey from the Inferno towards
Paradise Dante nears heaven, he hears a mighty sound. The
angels are singing the praises of God the Holy Trinity. For
in God's presence we can only worship. "It seemed to me,"
he says, "like the laughter of the universe." Laughter is not
only happiness. We laugh when we are on the edge of

weeping. Life's absurdities can bring us to near hysteria. The cowering Orestes will laugh with relief, For the moment to be saved is to know enough of God to be able to struggle with him and on behalf of others in his world worship him. But our hope remains, along with Dante, that one day we shall be finally saved and then share in all these sorts of laughter which make up the "laughter of the universe".

FOR DISCUSSION

1. Does the distinction between sin and evil help you in making some sense of life today?

2. How does the cross test your church's life and worship? What will you do about it?

3. What through this Lent has caused you laughter? Is it in any sense part of the "laughter of the universe"?

NOTES

CHAPTER 1

1. Thomas A. Harris (Jonathan Cape, London 1973). The book is a practical guide to Transactional Analysis.
2. Philo, *Special Laws*, 2.63.
3. *American Psycho* (Picador, London 1991), p. 399.
4. *The Stature of Waiting* (Darton, Longman and Todd, London 1982), p. 2.
5. Edwin Muir, "The Transfiguration", *Collected Poems* (Faber, London 1960), p. 198.

CHAPTER 2

1. Fiddes, *op. cit.*, p. 180.
2. Faber & Faber, London 1959.
3. Fiddes, *op. cit.*, p. 180.
4. Hamlet, 2.2.586–90.
5. *Scandalous Risks* (Fontana, London 1991), P. 422.
6. James Gleick, *Chaos* (Sphere, London 1987), p. 8.
7. Micheal O'Siadhail, "Perspectives", *The Chosen Garden* (Daedalus Press, Dublin 1990), p. 6.
8. See n.1.

CHAPTER 3

1. John Sweet, *Revelation* (SCM Press, London 1979), p. 48.
2. "Do not go gentle into that good night", in *Collected Poems* (J. M. Dent, London 1977), p. 207.
3. Alice L. Eckardt & A. Roy Eckardt, *Long Night's Journey into Day: A Revised Retrospective on the Holocaust* (Wayne State University Press,

Detroit and Pergamon Press, Oxford 1988), p. 115. The story of the woman is cited from Edward H. Flannery, *The Anguish of the Jews* (Paulist Press, New York 1985), p. xi.

4. Emil Fackenheim, "Jewish Values in the Post-Holocaust Future", *Judaism* 16 (1967), pp. 266–99, quoted in Eckhardt p. 78.

5. Wilfred Owen, "At a Calvary near Ancre", *The Poems of Wilfred Owen*, (Chatto & Windus, London 1985), p. 111.

CHAPTER 4

1. "The Future of TV Evangelism", *TV Guide* 31.10 (1983), quoted in Neil Postman, *Amusing Ourselves to Death* (Methuen, London 1986), p. 120.

2. Lewis Carroll, *Alice in Wonderland* (Oxford 1865), ch. 6.

3. E. Schweizer, *Jesus*, (SCM, London 1971), p. 45.

4. Eckhardt, *op. cit.*, p. 80 and n. 14.

5. D. W. Winnicott, quoted in Wesley Carr, *The Pastor as Theologian*, (SPCK, London 1990), p. 22.

6. R. S. Thomas, "Pilgrimages" in *Later Poems, 1972–1982* (Macmillan, London 1983), pp. 125–6.

7. A.-M. Rizzuto, *The Birth of the Living God* (Chicago University Press, Chicago 1979), p. 203.

8. Moltmann, *op. cit.*, p. 205. This sounds very twentieth century, but he is following a much older tradition from Gregory of Nyssa in the fourth century.

CHAPTER 5

1. Moltmann, *The Crucified God*, (SCM, London 1974), pp. 244 and 246. The quotation is from Luther: No one contradicts God, except God himself.

2. Wilfred Owen, "The Parable of the Old Man and the Young", *op. cit.*, p. 151.

3. Helen Waddell, *Peter Abelard* (Fontana, London 1958), pp. 240 ff. The book was first published in 1933.

4. This "heresy" linked the idea of God's suffering to the persons of

the Trinity. While the Son could suffer, classical thought denied that the Father could since, if God suffered, he would not be impassible – that is – incapable of being affected by events and feelings. If he was so touched, then he could be changed and would not be God.

5. From *Solus ad victimam procedis*, tr. F. Bland Tucker. BBC Hymn Book No. 79, London.

6. John Bunyan, *The Pilgrim's Progress*, ed. N. H. Keeble (OUP, Oxford 1984). p. 31.